UNLEASH YOUR DREAM HOME

By Gene Maida, MBA

HOME IS WHERE THE HEART IS

Selected by Jeanne Beker to expertly refresh and renovate her home, Georgian Renovations has been passionately committed to creating spaces you'll love for over 50 years. Whether it's a full-floor renovation, addition, or custom home, a **5-year exclusive warranty and fixed-price guarantee** ensure your complete satisfaction. See what Georgian can do for your home.

GEORGIAN RENOVATIONS
50 YEARS
GEORGIANRENO.COM

GEORGIAN®
RENOVATIONS

Put A Little Love In Your Home.

BOOK YOUR COMPLIMENTARY CONSULTATION TODAY AT **GEORGIANRENO.COM**

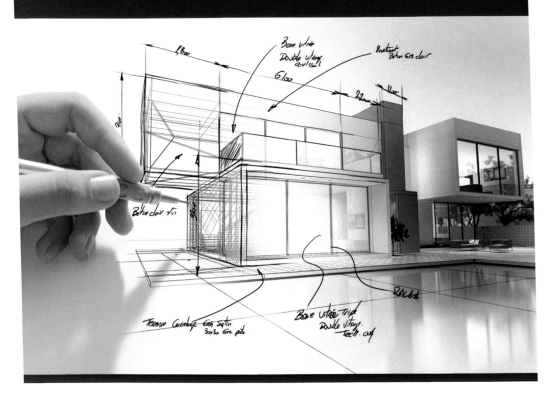

Inspire...Create...Perform

NATURAL
STONE
ELEGANCE

The Art Shoppe.
A Toronto icon since 1936.

Flatiron Building

Artfully inspired furniture you won't find anywhere else. Styles from traditional to modern and everyting in between. **The One. The Only.**

the *Art Shoppe*

Now at 71 Kincort Street

West of Caledonia & Castlefield   www.theartshoppe.com

DECORIUM®

YOUR HOME. **DESIGNED.**

At Decorium, we are passionate about quality, style and service. Offering an exceptional range of new and timeless pieces, paired with our industry leading designers, we make it easier than ever to style your home - fit just for you. After all, it's what you deserve.

Custom Furniture
Room Planning
Small Space Solutions
Free Design Consultation

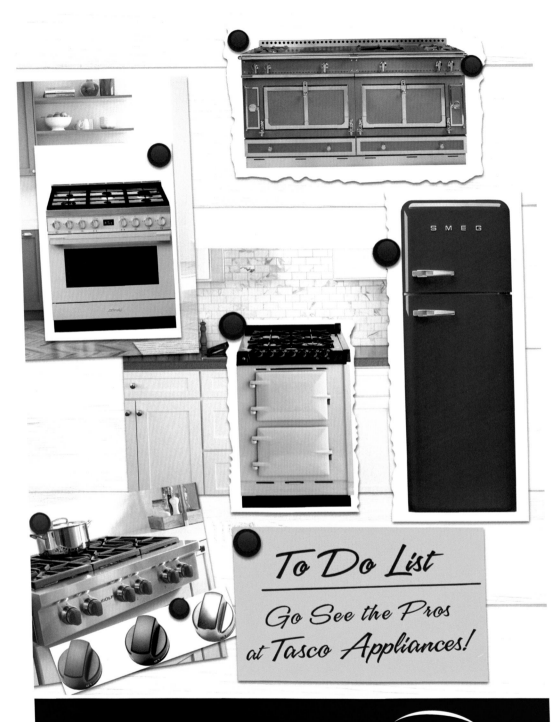

Floor Art

≈≈

"Great design will forever change your perspective…"

THE PURVEYOR

Michael Pourvakil
Owner of Weavers Art

EXCLUSIVE TO
WEAVERS ART

"This award-winning design
by Erbil Tezcan depicts the
quiet serenity which exists in
nature. The harmony of colours,
coupled with the randomness
of mother nature, makes for a
perfect canvas with which to
create this stunning design.
Hand-knotted in a blend of
Tibetan wool & silk, the soft
tones and vibrant accents
cohabit together in this design
as they do along rolling terrains
and lapping waters.

Visit our flagship showroom at
1400 Castlefield Ave, Toronto."

Tel: 416.929.7929
Web: www.weaversart.com

Snow – Original in Wool & Silk

WEAVERS ART
HOME TO THE WORLD'S MOST BEAUTIFUL RUGS™

SMART
ENTERTAINMENT
SOLUTIONS
The Ultimate Audio, Video and Lighting Experience

The final Touch in a Job Well Done

Top off your renovation with the most important step for functionality and beauty. Let one of our lighting consultants help you choose from an incredible selection of lamps, track lights, fans, chandeliers, pendants, outdoor lights, undercounter lights, garden lights recessed lights and more.

PS: Don't wait until the end!

preferred supplier of

GEORGIAN®
RENOVATIONS

ROYAL LIGHTING

1549 Avenue Rd. (North of Lawrence) 416•782•1129 royallighting.com

GEORGIAN®

RENOVATIONS

For over 50 years, Georgian Renovations has been renovating homes
with unparalleled craftsmanship, specializing in whole-floor and
whole-home renovations, additions and complete custom homes.

BOOK YOUR DESIGN CONSULTATION TODAY AT

GEORGIANRENO.COM

CONTENTS

FOREWARD BY JEANNE BEKER

The prospect of change can be an exhilarating one. But for many of us, it can also be terrifying—especially when it comes to altering our 'nests'. I equate the notion of home renovation to getting a personal makeover: We crave a new look, but we're often locked into certain images of ourselves. And because we may harbour closets stuffed with insecurities, we seldom venture out of our comfy style boxes. That's because sticking to what's familiar—though it may not always work perfectly for us—simply feels safer. The devil you know is better than the devil you don't know, right? Theoretically perhaps. But there's also something to be said about the frustration and foolhardiness of trying to put square pegs into round holes.

Face it: A lot of us are occupying homes we've outgrown, inhabiting spaces that no longer work for us, excite us, inspire us, please us, or make our lives any easier. But real change can be a scary process, and requires the kind of trusted guidance and expertise that isn't easy to come by. And because change can be so understandably emotional, it also demands compassion and understanding from those on the outside who are helping us find our way.

Besides the no-nonsense, savvy advice, insights and ideas that you'll find in these pages, I think you'll also find that sensitive friend you've been looking for—someone with the solid experience, wisdom and caring necessary to encourage you to dream and turn your vision into a stunning new reality.

Gene Maida understands us: He knows what busy, multi-faceted lives we lead, and how hard we work to keep it all together. He's also hip to the fact that, big or small, our homes really are our castles. If there's one thing that fuels Gene Maida's fire, it's his passion for making fairy tales come true.

So ladies—meet your new knight in shining armour! Living 'happily ever after' is about to get a whole lot easier...

Jeanne Beker

FOREWARD BY CHERYL HICKEY

If you're considering remodeling your home, but can't quite take the first step, then I highly recommend *Getting the Renovation You Want for the Home You Love,* by Gene Maida. In his engaging writing style, he shares informative stories about families and individuals who've been through the trials and tribulations of home renovations.

You'll learn through these stories, and Gene's wealth of expertise, that there is a right way and a wrong way to renovate a home. He will help uncover what's blocking you from taking that important leap to creating your dream home. He will dispel myths around financing (yes you can afford it), contractors, architects and why fixing your current home makes more sense than purchasing a new one. You will also be armed with knowledge to make smart decisions that prevent unnecessary frustrations and potential disasters. Most important of all, his book will help you confidently progress from dreaming about your perfect home to living in it. I highly recommend reading this before any major home renovation!

Cheryl Hickey

DEDICATION

To the wonderful women in my life, who are wondering if I wrote about them in this book: the answer is yes.

To my family who, without their loving support and understanding, I would have written this book one year earlier.

———

NOTES TO READER
Please write in this book.

This book is meant to be interactive and I want you to use this book as a handbook. Highlight things that interest you or things for your partner to read.

Answer the questions at the end of each chapter. Take the quizzes and make notes about your home or lifestyle.

Put the book away for a while and absorb all the ideas. Allow what you learned to be absorbed. Come back to your notes and write down how you feel about yourself and how this book has changed you.

Lastly, refer this book to someone you care about.

INTRODUCTION

"Home is where the heart is." – Old Proverb

The home is the gathering place for family to connect and feel secure, and the motivation to undergo a home renovation is typically to enrich that experience of connection, security, and comfort even more.

After years of meeting with families and discussing their renovation plans I've decided to write this book because I want to help homeowners avoid the struggles that often accompany a renovation and potentially lead to problems with the family or marriage.

It's my experience that the idea of a home renovation is daunting for most people. Homeowners can be skeptical, distrusting, and suffer from numerous disempowering and limiting beliefs about the home improvement process.

From my own research, fewer than 10% of people who read this book will actually proceed to perform a major renovation or project. The readers who do proceed may have a very stressful experience. 33% of homeowners who have completed a renovation stated that the project caused tension with their partners and among the families they live with. In fact, 15% of those surveyed said they considered separation or divorce upon the completion of the project. I will provide some useful tips to ensure your renovation journey is enjoyable.

I want to help ensure homeowners achieve a successful renovation while maintaining strong family bonds during and after the renovation. I've decided to write this book because I want to help homeowners avoid the struggles that often accompany a renovation and potentially lead to problems with the family or marriage.

What You'll Learn in This Book

I want to dispel the myths around the renovation business and provide homeowners with the skills and knowledge to attain their dream homes while avoiding major blunders. I use the technique of storytelling to make learning easier and more fun. The stories reflect the many experiences I've had visiting wonderful families in their homes across the GTA. While the anecdotal stories are based on fictional characters, they accurately represent the situations I've experienced with various families, couples, and individuals over the years.

After completing renovations, homeowners with whom I've worked reported the following:

80% feel more relaxed

84% spend more time in their home

55% entertain more in their home

71% report they're happier in their home

50% report that their children are healthier and happier

50% report their children are more likely to attend post-secondary school, have successful careers, lead healthier and more fulfilling lives, and live longer

66% experienced better learning and memory capabilities when their home is uncluttered

Customers make renovations for any number of personal reasons, such as pleasure, ego, status, security, belonging, safety, betrayal, frustration, privacy, and avoiding embarrassment. Psychologists explain that customers renovate based on emotions and then justify the decision intellectually. The bottom line is that customers buy to eliminate problems that cause them pain. Pain, by definition, is a problem that somebody wants solved. People do not buy because of benefits, they buy because of the gap between where they are and where they want to be. By simply talking to them and getting to know them a little, I help customers feel comfortable enough to discover their actionable emotional pains.

The discussion step is important because, let's face it, a renovation is a scary prospect that has many people run for cover. That's the emotional response: making decisions based on feelings and justifying those decisions with one's own brand of logic. Far too often, I hear people back out of a renovation project with statements such as "The whole thing is too scary!" or "I'm going to get screwed over!" or "I can't afford it, it's too messy!"

In Mel Robbins' book *The 5 Second Rule,* Robbins explains that the moment customers have an instinct to act on a goal, they hesitate and feel fear. The primal subconscious brain kicks in to protect customers. It reinforces the fear with ideas and images that will cause pain if a certain action is taken. This is an automatic subconscious reaction, also known as a "terror barrier". Robbins recommends that we find the courage to do things that feel difficult or scary by practicing the five second rule –counting backwards from five to zero, and then taking the action required.

I help customers break through this terror barrier. Later on in this book, I will discuss how we are often held back by our subconscious and how it influences our decisions through fears. I will also explore how we make decisions based on inherited ideas and outdated beliefs that have been passed down to us from previous generations.

As I said earlier, only 10% of brave homeowners will break through their terror barriers and open up their minds and wallets in order to get the dream home they always wanted. The others will continue to live in denial and suffer without their dream home, throwing money away on stop-gap repairs.

I will explore what it means to be happy and how we are able to achieve it. This will include a description of the six fundamental needs we try to fulfill in our everyday lives, based on the writings of Tony Robbins and Cloé Madanes. I further explain how to overcome the limiting beliefs that prevent many people from making the choices that can lead to happiness. I have come to recognize that these concepts are directly correlated to the homeowner's choice to renovate or not.

The final chapter pulls all the pieces together to create an ideal renovation process and result. I will share the core motivation behind every renovation project that a typical family undertakes. This motivation is so powerful that it can break through years of ambiguity, indecisiveness, and paralysis. You will learn how homeowners can undo years of programming and limiting beliefs to break through terror barriers and proceed with the renovation of their dreams.

This book is an homage to nesting, the most basic of human needs. Rather than leapfrogging from one home to the next, homeowners are increasingly staying put and revitalizing what they already know and love. I hope this book will empower you to change your home and lifestyle for the better.

The valuable secrets and tips within these pages will save you thousands of dollars and make your renovation journey seamless and enjoyable. – Gene

Chapter 1

Why We Hate Salespeople!

"Of course it's cheating! Nobody ever got rich by being honest."

– Danny DeVito as Mr. Wormwood in Matilda

There's a moment in every parent's life that they dread from the day that they bring their babies home from the hospital. A single sentence, a few simple words that change everything.

"Daddy, I want you to buy me a car."

It's a dilemma many parents find themselves in: should you buy your child's first car, or have them save the money on their own?

My son hadn't saved any money, but when he turned 16, he became what child psychology experts call "car crazy".

For any teenager, buying your first car is a big deal. My son had been hammering and pestering me for over three months up until that point. It wasn't just for the sake of having one: he needed transportation to get to and from school on his own.

"C'mon, Dad," he said, "all of my friends' parents bought them cars. Why can't you?"

Now, as a full-time single dad, I was speechless.

After the divorce, I became something of a "Disney Dad", always wanting to do anything for my son. Usually, this involved spoiling him rotten to some degree. Still, a car? That was a big ask, but here he was, asking.

"Dad, I've been looking at cars for months now," he said to me. "I'm really excited. Please, can we go get one?" The look in his eyes was so hopeful, and I felt guilty.

Was I being played? Probably, but it didn't matter. In the end, I didn't want my son to be known among his buddies as the "car disadvantaged" friend.

On top of that, I didn't want an old Junker sitting in my driveway.

"All right," I said to him. "Here's what we'll do. We'll go look at cars together-"

My son jumped just about five feet in the air, cheering. "Yes!"

"But," I said, waiting for him to calm down, "not until the first weekend of June. I think this will be a learning experience for you. You'll be able to experience the process of buying a car, and you'll get to learn how to take pride in taking care of a vehicle. It'll be good for you to see exactly what it takes to own a car."

"That's great, Dad, thanks!" he said, giving me a hug. "I'm really excited!" "Yeah, don't get too excited," I cautioned, looking him square in the eye. "We're just going to look. We're not going to buy anything, okay?"

Famous last words.

A few weeks later, on that first Saturday in June, my son and I found ourselves at one of the biggest car dealerships in our area. We were barely on the property for thirty seconds when a salesman pounced on us.

"Good morning!" he said. "How are you today?"

I sized him up. Late thirties guy, brown hair, slight pot-belly protruding behind his blue collared shirt and red tie. Name tag said "Dave". What stood out the most was that he spoke at this really break-neck speed like an auctioneer from the Old South.

A fast-talking car salesman named Dave. Just my luck.

"We've got a few promotions happening just this weekend, " said Dave breathlessly. He gestured outside. "As you probably saw coming in, there's a lot of inventory on our hands, so you have a lot of selection and I can find something within your budget. How much are you looking to spend today?"

At this, I said nothing. No way was I going to tell him my budget and lose my leveraging power (assuming I had any). You never give the salesman your figure: they'll do everything they can to muscle you into spending more.

Of course, my son didn't know that. Before I could tell Dave that we were just looking, he piped up.

"We're interested in the Acura MDX that you've got priced at $30,000," he said. "Can we see that one?"

Dave looked away from me and focused on my son, who was very enthusiastic about all the attention he was getting. They'd known each other for a grand total of 2 minutes and already they were BFF (or whatever word for "friends" kids are using these days).

"Such a great car, isn't it?" replied Dave, then he shrugged slightly. "Unfortunately, we just sold that one yesterday, I'm really sorry. But, I can show you some other models that are just as good, if not better, than the MDX. Do you wanna see?"

My son looked at me, clearly ready to do some shopping. I wanted to remind him right then and there that we were just looking, that I was skeptical that the Acura MDX they had advertised had actually even been there, and that the whole thing might have been a bait-and-switch designed to get us to the dealership. Still, I saw that same gleam of hope in my son's eyes and felt that same pang of guilt. Disney Dad, in full force.

We followed Dave out to the parking lot (which was just full of unsold cars) while Dave himself just droned on and on and on. "This is the thing about the MDX," he said. "It's kind of an old man's car-"He glanced up at me. "I mean, no offense, sir!" I smiled grudgingly, and my son laughed and clapped me on the back (he was just loving this!). "What you really want is the Acura TL. It's a bit sportier and age-appropriate."

He brought us to the TL, which was painted red and looked pretty impressive. "The TL's got a turbocharged V6 engine and 350 horse power. Really sporty, perfect for a young man getting his first car."

"Hmm..." said my son. "Does it come in white? I'm looking for a white car".

Dave chuckled, and then shrugged. "I figured you would! White is in big demand, so they're pretty scarce right now. If you were to buy today, though, I'd do everything in my power to get you a white TL."

That wasn't right. I looked around the lot. There were a lot of white cars of various makes and models sitting around. Dave was clearly lying about the demand for white cars, and something told me that lie wasn't going to be the first one.

"What about all those ones?" I asked him. Dave glanced over and then ignored my question completely, focusing back on my son. "Besides, the TLs are in big demand and do not depreciate. There's a big after-market demand for them, but on this one, there's a lot of features. Do you want to hear some of them?"

My son nodded with an enthusiasm I hadn't seen since his last gift from Santa Claus. We listened as Dave rattled off the features of the Acura TL and, in doing so, capturing my son's imagination:

Six speed automatic transmission *not too bad*

Power sunroof *neato!*

Dual-zone automatic climate control *not bad*

A state-of-the-art sound system with rear speakers that Dave said, "will make you the envy of all your friends." (better throw in some noise-cancelling headphones for Dad, Dave).

All leather seats *terrific!*

GPS *not bad*

17-inch alloy wheels with carbon brakes *okay*

ABS system *isn't this standard on most cars today?*

Tilt telescopic steering wheel ... *huh?*

5

"And all for the low, low price of $59,000!" said Dave proudly, before gesturing back to the TL in front of us. "Now, I do have a fully-loaded car that has these features that is painted white, but I've taken it off the floor. Another family was looking at it earlier and they promised to come back tomorrow to buy it."

My son shook his head, crestfallen. "Awe, that's too bad."

Guilt once again swelled up in my cheeks. I took a breath and asked my question. "Is that $59,000 price tag negotiable?"

Dave looked at me, his own smirking expression now a mix of friendliness and regret and shook his head. "No sir," he said, "we don't negotiate prices here."

"Okay, but if I were to get a cheaper quote from another dealership, would you beat it?"

Dave shook his head again, emphatically. "No dealership is allowed to discount their prices, or they would lose their dealership."

Another lie. Just a straight up lie, told right to our faces.

"Here," continued Dave, oblivious to the vein above my right eye that was starting to throb, "we have the best financing. In fact, we had this great $300 a month financing deal, but it just ended in May. Tell you what, though: if you were to pick up this car today, I could pull some strings with my boss and get that deal for you".

Dave stopped, as if gripped by a sudden idea. "Actually, please follow me, gentlemen!"

We walked back into the showroom to Dave's office. "Please have a seat! I'm just going to go talk to my manager and see what I can arrange for you." Before I could say anything, Dave stepped out.

My son sat down in front of Dave's desk, eyes still beaming with excitement. "Isn't Dave awesome, Dad?" I opened my mouth to say something but didn't want to dim his light. I sat down and checked messages on my phone.

A couple of minutes later, Dave returned, paperwork in hand. "Good news!" he said. "I went to my manager and explained how you were both very interested in the TL and that you were great people, so he made an exception in this case and gave you last month's financing deal. In fact, if you sign the paperwork today, I'll also throw in some floor mats and detailing right from my own pocket."

"Wow! Dave, that's amazing!" said my son. "That's so awesome of you, dude! Dad, what do you think?'

Dave did seem to be going to bat for us. "Remind me again, that was $300 a month, right?"

"Absolutely! As long as you can pay the $10,000 down today, you can get the low monthly financing rate. That was the deal." He handed me the paperwork, which he's somehow managed to print up out of our sight while also talking to his manager.

Dave had failed to mention a $10,000 down payment before.

I skimmed the first two pages while Dave and my son waited. There it was, $10,000 down. What else could be in there? Still, I couldn't focus with two sets of eyes on me.

"I want to take this home with me and read it first," I said.

"I wouldn't worry about it," replied Dave. "That's a standard contract and we don't allow changes. Everyone just signs it."

I think my son was ready to explode at this point. "See, Dad? It's standard. Why bother reading it?"

Before I could answer, Dave snapped his fingers "Oh, I almost forgot." He turned back to my son. "Since you'll be a first-time car owner, I highly recommend the extended warranty. It'll make sure that any little scrapes or even big problems that you might run into as a new driver, you'll get bumper-to-bumper coverage. It's only an extra $5,000. Whatever happens to your car, we'll fix it, no questions asked."

"That makes sense," said my son, nodding emphatically.

(Later, I'd discover that most of those extended warranty policies ask you a lot of questions before they'll cover your repairs. Always read the fine print!).

Finally, Dave went in for the kill. "As I said, I like you guys and want to help you out. Here's the thing: my manager's going home in an hour, and the terms are only good while he's here." He then looked at me. "Will the $10,000 down be on Visa or Mastercard?" He said nothing more.

My son, too, just stared at me, a hint of desperation now creeping across his face, his agreement that we were "just here to look" a forgotten memory in the distant past.

Now I really felt backed into a corner. Dave was clearly strong-arming me and had managed to enroll my son in his sales approach. Though I knew better, I now had this itchy little fear in my subconscious, a feeling that said if I didn't buy this car today, it would be gone tomorrow.

I looked again at the contract. Despite all of the manipulation and blatant lies, Dave had managed to leverage me. My son had to have this car, a car I had not intended on buying, that was way too expensive, that I would have likely found for a lesser price if I'd looked elsewhere, and that had way more than what he needed, and Dave knew it.

I sighed. "Can I have a pen?" Dave grinned like the devil, handed me the ballpoint on his desk.

"Of course! And congratulations! You've made all the right moves today!"

The Brutal, Honest Truth

I hate salespeople!
There, I said it.

From the fast-talking car salesman to the door-to-door solicitor hawking everything from heating contracts to religion, I detest them the second they open their mouths. I am immediately wary of their manipulation techniques and the fake, sly smile that's plastered all over their faces. It's clear that their only goal is to make the sale, regardless of whether I need the product or service.

I know I'm not alone in my opinion. Many people have the fear that a salesperson will talk them into doing something that is not right for them, doesn't meet their needs or doesn't create real value. We're fearful of making a foolish purchase, and even worse, overpaying for it.

When this does happen (we've all been there), we regretfully admit that the salesperson didn't listen to us, understand our needs and pressured us into saying yes to something we didn't want or need. No surprise, then, that buyers are often guarded when a salesperson approaches them.

Why do I dislike salespeople so much? If I haven't yet made myself clear, here are my top five reasons:

- Lack of transparency: The motivation to make the sale supersedes all else. Important details about the product or service are purposely kept hidden from the customer.

- Lack of trust: The customer feels like the salesperson will say anything just to make a sale.

- Broken promises: The failure of salespeople to follow through on promises and an overall lack of knowledge.

- Misrepresenting the product or service: They mislead customers and overstate the benefits of the product by stretching the truth or by providing wrong information.

- Not listening: The salesperson talks too much and doesn't listen to the customer.

I started my professional career in my dad's construction business back when I was barely out of my teens. I pledged that I would never be a salesperson or work in sales in any way. I would never allow myself to become a shady businessman who makes a living by tricking people into buying products or services that they don't need.

However, that thinking started to change when I better understood what "selling" really meant.

Maybe I'm being harsh. If you're a salesperson, you're probably thinking: "C'mon, Gene, why are you so hard on us? Our intentions are generally honorable. Stop giving us such a bad rap and encouraging others to question our motives!"

You're right, I'm generalizing. I know that not all salespeople are bad. But I do know that many of them could learn a thing or two about getting it right. Making a sale should not be based on high-pressure sales tactics, lying, cheating, or anything else underhanded. Rather, it should be based on gathering intelligence about the customer and asking the right questions. This would help prevent an adversarial relationship from developing between the prospect and the person trying to close the sale.

At its most basic level, sales is simply interacting with people. In fact, we are all salespeople in some fashion. It starts when we are children as we attempt to convince our parents to buy us the latest toy or let us stay up late. Sales, in fact, is part of our daily lives, from the local butcher promoting organic beef to a political candidate running for office, and even the search for a romantic partner.

When done right, a good sales job bridges the gap between a customer's needs and the products or services that fulfill that need. It's an opportunity to create an authentic relationship with customers and provide real value where and when it counts.

The Honest Sales Approach

When I entered this business, I wanted to make a difference in my customers' lives. I saw shortcomings in the way renovations were managed and realized there was a better way. I am proud to be an honest salesperson!

My approach is simple and straightforward. I ask the customers questions, listen to their answers and help them discover their actionable emotional reasons to buy. It is based on the following five key principles:

1. Be transparent and caring
2. Create trust
3. Keep promises
4. Tell the truth
5. Listen to customers

I take the time to know my customers and learn why they want to renovate. I engage customers in a meaningful conversation to discover the problems with their homes. I discuss whether or not my service is well-suited for them. If we're not a good fit, I let them know. I don't want to waste a customer's valuable time and hard-earned money.

Once I've determined the relationship is a good fit, I begin a thorough assessment of the renovation project. How do I do this? I talk to the customers to determine why they're considering a renovation in the first place. Customers are encouraged to be honest and to share as much information as possible so that I can develop a deep understanding of their goals and objectives. I want to examine the "why" behind the project, determine a realistic timeline and price range for it, and ensure there is 100% commitment to turn their dream into a reality.

Questions to consider

○ Why are you deciding to renovate?
What is the desired outcome that you want to have from a renovation?

○ What qualities do you want in a service provider

○ What are some of the fears that you want your service provider to address before you decide to renovate?

Chapter 2

History By Design

"Oh if this Old House could talk What a story it would tell..."

– Loretta Lynn

Last Christmas, my friends Heidi and Ian invited me to their place for dinner during the holidays. Heidi is Jewish and Ian is Catholic, so they decided to celebrate Hanukkah and Christmas together with friends of both faiths.

I was intrigued. Would the tree be decorated with a menorah or Christmas lights, or both? Would the cookies for Santa be kosher?

Heidi and Ian live in Rosedale, an affluent Toronto neighbourhood located just north of the downtown core. It's one of the city's oldest suburbs and is particularly noted for its stunning period architecture including historic red-brick mansions dating from the Victorian and Edwardian eras of the late 1800s and early 1900s. With stately broad tree-lined avenues, lush ravines and manicured front lawns, it's easy to see why Rosedale is such a fashionable address.

As I approached the three-story home, I was impressed with the large front yard framed with an interlock driveway and beautiful landscaping. I was in awe of the height of the house as I climbed the stairs to the elegant porch. The majestic stone walls were breathtaking, with intriguing columns and exceptional detail around the wood windows that felt right out of Gone with the Wind.

I could hear the seasonal music coming from inside the house as I passed through the front door. No Dreidel Song yet! It was definitely Bing Crosby's greatest hits.

"Gene! Great to see you, buddy!" bellowed Ian as soon as he saw me, his ugly reindeer sweater practically screaming rum-and-eggnog. "Come on in! It's been such a long time. Whatcha been up to? How are the kids? How's the business going? Come in, make yourself at home! We're so happy you could make it. What can I get you to drink?"

He was still chattering as I handed him a bottle of pretty decent pinot noir and followed him down the hallway. On the way, I was instantly drawn to the pile of coats thrown over the front hall bannister...

that meant there was a small front hall closet (I can't help it – I'm in the renovation business so I notice these things.) I took in the impressive wood wainscoting on the wall and up the staircase with the matching railing and pickets. The baseboards and window casing had unique dove-tail wooden joints. The high ceilings evoked a sense of grandeur.

We entered the spacious kitchen, where Ian's wife was chatting with several guests as she removed a dish from the oven.

"Gene! How lovely to see you!" she said as she set a hot tray on the stovetop and turned to the other guests.

"Everyone, this is my friend Gene, the renovator extraordinaire I was telling you about. Gene, this is everyone!"

The conversation flowed easily once we all introduced ourselves. There were two lawyers, a pediatrician, a real estate agent, and two stock brokers, one of whom told some amusing "tales" about his elite Rosedale clients.

As I listened to the chitchat, my eyes wandered. I noticed that the original solid wide-plank wood floor extended from the front hallway, living room, and dining room right into the kitchen. I was impressed by the elaborate plaster ceiling moldings and the amazing chandelier hanging from upstairs into the front hallway. I could feel the warmth emanating from the wood burning fireplace in the living room.

Soon, I was roaming around the house. Confession: I really wished I could tiptoe upstairs without anyone knowing (don't worry, I didn't). I guiltily felt like one of those guests who snoop inside the medicine cabinet when they're using the bathroom. Good thing my renovations don't include medicine cabinets any longer.

The more I looked (okay, snooped), the more apparent it became that the house had not been touched in years. Virtually everything was original: the knob-and-tube wiring, hot-water radiators, dated kitchen cupboards. The wallpaper in the living room was almost identical to the one my grandmother had in her den! For a second I felt like I was walking onto the set of my favorite Christmas film, Miracle on 34th Street.

While I appreciate the nostalgic appeal of these old homes, behind the beautiful façade, there's usually a train wreck waiting to happen thanks to outdated plumbing, wiring, heating, insulation, windows, roofing, and foundation problems. In Heidi and Ian's case, the floor plan was awkward and felt disconnected from their lifestyle. For instance, the powder room was tucked under the staircase with a low ceiling height. It was so small, that once I got inside there was no turning back!

Okay, I'm exaggerating, but still, it's a common feature in Victorian houses like this. In the 18th century, it was fashionable for men to wear wigs and they needed a private room to powder their wigs when their head got sweaty (really!). The rooms didn't need plumbing or much space. But today's powder rooms are meant for grander things. To me, Heidi and Ian's just wouldn't do.

As I emerged from the powder room, thankful that I still had a full head of hair, I caught sight of the bright red sweater making its way towards me.

"There you are, Gene!" exclaimed Ian, letting out a laugh. "We thought you might be upstairs already, going through the medicine cabinets."

Was this guy psychic or what?

I followed him down the hallway to join the ensemble at the dining room table. By the end of our turkey dinner and second glass of wine, the banter was flowing and festive. The realtor turned out to be Heidi's lifelong friend, Penny, who sat beside her. I sat beside Ian and Penny's husband, one of the lawyers. Beside him sat James, the well-dressed stock broker. He lived next door with his partner,

Johnny, who had gone out of town to spend some time with his parents.

It didn't take long before the conversation turned to holiday decorating and entertaining. James led the conversation. Turns out he and Johnny had gutted their century-old home next door and enlarged it with an addition. By his own admission, it was "sophisticated" and "elaborate" and "utterly fabulous" for hosting dinner parties. He insisted that it had definitely been worth the time, money and aggravation. Then he turned on his hosts.

"You've got to do it," he gushed. "This place of yours would be ideal for a reno of awesome proportions. Imagine what an utterly fabulous kitchen you'd have. I can see it now. A walkout to that gorgeous back garden of yours, a kitchen island that looks into the den, a splashy powder room instead of that tiny one down the hall, a front closet that actually has rooms for coats ... isn't that right, Gene?"

Instantly, all eyes were on me. Cringe! But before I could respond, Ian took the floor (phew!).

"We've talked about it," he said, glancing sheepishly at Heidi. "In fact, we've shouted about it, too. We love this place and we know it needs an update, but it's overwhelming thinking about the upheaval it would bring. We've had endless conversations about what to do and how to do it. But we just can't agree. You know, I read somewhere that renovations put more stress on a marriage than having a new baby. We've got a great marriage going for 26 years now but I'm not sure it could survive a long construction project!"

Ian laughed, but the rest of us were all squirming in our seats, especially Heidi. Thankfully, James took the floor once more.

James asked me "Gene you are the expert here, can you enlighten us about why these Victorian homes have such an awkward floor plan? What were they thinking when they designed a powder room under the staircase with such low head room?"

I took a deep breath as everyone in the room started to focus their attention on me. I responded, treading carefully for fear of insulting my hosts. "Part of the problem of these century old homes is the they were designed by men who knew nothing about how woman wanted to live in them. " That comment got a big laugh from the women around the table. I went on to explain how home design treads had evolved over time.

The New Home of the Modern Age

There's no doubt that houses built a century ago, like Heidi and Ian's, have redeeming qualities. But they reflect the lifestyle of the early 1900s when men were the breadwinners and women managed the household. Refrigerators had not been invented yet so Mom shopped every day for fresh food. Milk and bread were delivered daily right to the front door which meant no need for large kitchens. There was no air conditioning so families hung out on the porch, which often wrapped around the house. People entertained in the front parlor or gathered there to listen to comedy shows and news on the radio. There was no need for large closets. Carpets were scarce because they were too hard to clean without vacuum cleaners. Few families had cars, so who needed a garage?

While we're on the subject of cars, my Dad had a red two-door Dodge Dart with windows that we had to physically roll down, locks that we had to pull up or push down, an AM radio and an eight-track player. Boy, how things have changed! Cars have become easier to drive with automatic transmissions, power steering, power brakes, ABS braking systems, the works! Doors and windows are automatic, navigation systems tell you where to go. There's cruise control, in-dash phones, back-seat entertainment systems. Cars are much safer, with as many as 10 air bags, accident avoidance features such as collision warning systems, blind-spot recognition and alert sensors. There are fuel-efficient models, hybrids, electric cars, even self-driving cars! In short, car manufacturers have designed vehicles that suit our modern lifestyle.

Back in the day, basements were hand-dug so it was expensive to go very deep, which is why houses were built six feet above the ground with stairs to the main floor. The structure was built out of solid masonry and the walls and roof were all hand-cut from spruce lumber. They were poorly insulated and built with plaster walls and ceilings. All of them still had hot water heating, an oil tank and dangerous knob-and-tube wiring.

The post-war baby-boom years and the rise of the personal automobile fueled the rapid rise of the suburbs. One of the first major suburban development was at Don Mills in North York. Founded in 1952, it was the first master-planned community in Canada and it initiated many practices that would become standard in Toronto suburbs. Suburbs like Scarborough, Etobicoke, Pickering, Mississauga, Markham, and Oakville grew incredibly quickly. In fact, Mississauga became so large so fast that it's now Canada's sixth largest city with 752,000 residents and more than 86,000 businesses, including more than 70 Fortune 500 companies with Canadian head offices or major divisional head offices.

With this kind of growth, developers embraced all the new technologies that allowed them to construct production homes with economies of scale. Powerful bulldozers and excavators allowed for deeper basements. Poured concrete foundation walls quickened construction times. Stick construction with brick veneer replaced solid masonry methods. State-of-the-art electrical wiring and central heating (either electric or gas) allowed for ever-expanding floor plans. Drywall replaced the archaic plaster. New building codes demanded better installation with vapor barriers, energy-efficient windows, tight air leakage ratings and efficient heating and lighting systems.

All this changed the look and feel of new homes, prompting purchasers to take notice. While a house in the mid-1970s was typically 1,500 sq. ft. and took more than a year to construct, by the late 1980s it took just six months to build a typical 3,000 sq. ft. home featuring the new standard: four bedrooms, a living room, dining room, kitchen and family room with a main floor laundry room.

Today's houses, increasingly found in new subdivisions, are equipped for life in the 21st Century. Increasingly open-concept, breakfast bars often supplanting dining rooms as more families (and an increasing number of single owners and childless couples) forgo eating together in favour of watching TV in the den or in their own rooms. Houses are built to up-to-date safety codes using modern wiring and environmentally-friendly materials and devices. And, within the next twenty to thirty years, they are likely to evolve again as society and culture continue to change.

Why am I sharing all of this with you? Simple: in today's housing market, the new builds may have a lot of good features to serve your needs, but they lack the character, roots, and distinctiveness of houses that are much older. On the other hand, if you move to an older house, you may inherit the problems that come with things like old plumbing, decaying walls and foundations, and so on (and that's if you can afford the older houses!). With the proper renovations to your existing home, you can have the best of both worlds: time-honoured character and distinctiveness combined with 21st century comfort, style, and safety. It's ultimately up to you.

Questions to consider

o Is your home organised or full of clutter?
Do you have room for entertaining?

o Is the layout of your home efficient or chopped
up and disconnected? Does your kitchen look
out to the family room and an open concept?

o Do you have enough storage?

o Are your heating, electrical and plumbing
systems up to code?

Chapter 3

Should You Stay or Should You Go?

"Darling, you've gotta let me know: should I stay or should I go?"

- The Clash

Love It, Don't List It

As I followed my GPS through the maze of streets to a customer's house, I found myself admiring the neighbourhood. The homes were beautiful! Judging by the manicured lawns and landscaping, it was clear that the homeowners were proud of their properties.

I visited this neighbourhood often over the years when my son played rep hockey at the local hockey rink. It has many alluring features: schools, parks, restaurants, convenience stores, major shopping malls, close proximity to the highway and much more. In real estate parlance, it possesses the three must-have features: location, location, location!

I rang the doorbell and was greeted by an attractive woman, who introduced herself as Eleanor, followed by a boy of about 10 who was trying desperately to hold back a giant, barking great dane (thank you, kid!). The woman, dressed in a black Lululemon outfit, was probably in her mid-40s and looked like she worked out regularly. After shushing the mammoth dog (whom she called "Oscar") we squeezed past him into the kitchen where I met her husband, Tom. We shook hands and settled in at the kitchen table.

"So," I said, turning to Eleanor after exchanging pleasantries. "How can I help you?"

She looked quickly at Tom and smiled, then turned to me. "We're really busy people," she began. "Tom practices law downtown, and I work at home as an accountant. We've got three kids, twin eleven-year-old boys who are just full of energy and a teenage girl who does competitive dancing. The boys play hockey in the winter and soccer in the summer, and we're always rushing around from one thing to the next." Eleanor took a breath before continuing. "We are constantly going from hockey arenas, soccer fields and dance studios, then over to my parents', who are getting on in age and need us to help them around their home."

Pausing, she looked around and sighed. "Managing this place isn't at the top of our priority list, and I don't think it's ever been. The whole house is disorganized and cluttered, and we barely have any storage space. Honestly, I'm fed up."

I nodded, just letting Eleanor vent, showing her obvious frustration. "So, when I called you, I mentioned the flood that we'd had in the basement, right?"

"That's right," I replied. "I'm sorry to hear about it."

Eleanor's hands clenched as she continued. "I was so embarrassed when the insurance adjuster came over to inspect the damage and he commented how old and outdated our finishes were. I realized that it was time for a complete update. The house feels completely dysfunctional."

She clasped her hands together and looked intently at me. "We need help, Gene."

I nodded my head. She wasn't the first person to seek my expertise out of desperation. It was time, however, for the home tour so that I could see for myself how serious this situation really was.

Having toured this style of house on many occasions, I knew exactly what to expect. A typical subdivision home, it had a center hall plan and circular staircase with dated wood pickets facing the front door. A powder room was adjacent to the staircase. The living room, dining room and cramped kitchen were situated on one side of the house and a family room, laundry room and mud room adjacent to the garage were on the other side.

My first impulse was to lift my arms in the air and announce, "You need a complete overhaul!" but I bit my tongue and tried not to wince as I took in the outdated parquet floors, the small baseboard, and casing around the doors and windows, the lack of lighting, the dated stipple ceiling, and the tired laminate kitchen countertops. As we walked upstairs, I cringed at the wear marks on the railing and the treads. The upper landing was awash with natural light, but the stipple ceiling was faded with water stains: the telltale sign of a past roof leak.

Once inside the master bedroom, Eleanor leaned in close. "Tom and I are having some problems in here," she says, glancing sadly around the room.

"Sorry to hear that, but I don't do that kind of work," I deadpan, then let out a laugh so she knew I was just having fun.

She looked at me quizzingly and then let out a chuckle. "Oh, Gene, not those kinds of problems! It's just that the room is draughty and cold at night and there's only so much cuddling we can do to stay warm in the dead of winter!"

"That's easy to fix," I said. "What else bothers you about the room?"

"Well, there's the closet ...," she replied, her face turning a slight crimson. "I'm too embarrassed to show you the closet. It's a mess."

"Hey, I'm a professional!" I replied. "Do you know how many closets I've seen? Some people come out of the closet. I go into them!"

Sure enough, the closet was a disaster. It was so small that things were shoved wherever there was room, with no rhyme or reason why things were where they were. Shoes piled upon boots, evening dresses squeezed up against hoodies and hat boxes. Tom had his own closet, but it didn't look much better. I could only imagine what the kids had done with theirs but, thankfully, she spared me the misery.

Then we moved to the ensuite bathroom. It was tidy, I'll give it that, but the layout was not ideal with its one lonely sink and a large built-in tub that dominates the room.

"Feeling any vibes?" Eleanor asked sheepishly.

Was I? I was feeling claustrophobic! There wasn't much I could do with this cramped floor plan, so I looked her in the eye and told her the truth.

"The bottom line is that you need more useable space, "I said. "To achieve that, I'd suggest an addition out over the roof of the three-car garage to create a new master bedroom with a spa-like ensuite and two large his-and-hers walk-in closets. We could design a whole new roof, offering up ten-foot ceilings in the bedroom. Believe me, it would be a fantastic space."

As I spoke, Eleanor's eyes lit up.

We maneuvered back to the kitchen. Eleanor saw my eyes fall on a huge pile of paperwork on one end of the counter. She blushed. "I have to admit," she said, "the kitchen is my home office, and my files are slowly taking over the room." (As if I couldn't tell?)

"I hadn't noticed," I deadpanned, and she chuckled. "Yeah, it's pretty bad. I even have magnetic file folders on the side of the fridge!"

"Hmmm," I said, trying not to look as frustrated as I felt. "Wouldn't it be more efficient if you set up your business in another room, like your own private office, and left the kitchen for cooking and socializing? We could knock down the walls between the family room, the dining room and the kitchen to open up the space and let the natural light flow throughout. With all the extra space you'll get in the kitchen, we could put in an island made of natural stone and then have a matching backsplash. Nice, eh?"

She smiled as her gaze drifted into a vision of her perfect home for a few seconds before she blinked out of it and turned back to me. "Lately, I've been dropping into open houses at new custom homes. I love those modern features. Tom and I had considered selling and buying new, but I can't convince the accountant in me to reconcile spending money on the same square footage that I already have."

Tom walked back into the kitchen just in time to hear Eleanor say "I'd really rather invest the same amount in this house than move and disrupt everyone's lives." Tom let out a huff.

"Really, Eleanor?" he said. "Are we going through this again? What's wrong with a new home? The new ones are better insulated and energy-efficient, they're open-concept, they have high-end finishes. And what's not to love about ten-foot ceilings instead of our eight-and-a-half-foot ones, especially for a tall guy like me?"

Tom looked at me, and went into his own breathless rant (who says opposites attract? Hook these two up to a generator when they're really talking and they could power all of North York for a week!).

"Gene," said Tom, "the other weekend we were driving by this great new subdivision in King City and we decided to take a look at the model home, just for fun. Man, was it ever spacious and nice. Even I could tell Eleanor was dazzled. But she doesn't want to let go of this place for some reason, and she doesn't want to be so far away from our family and friends and her clients. She's always going on about the larger mortgage we'd need as well as all the extra cash we'd have to put out for new drapery, TVs, landscaping and everything else that goes with buying new. I get it, but I'm so sick of living in this tired old place."

He took a breath then continued. "Last year, we had a 'Burn the Mortgage' party." I looked over at Eleanor, who nodded with a smile as Tom continued. "It's been a tremendous relief to be debt-free, so you can imagine when we started talking about buying a new house and starting the whole racket all over again that I was not really happy. We did some math and found that it would cost us more than $8,000 a month to get into one of those houses! I can't imagine that anyone would be eager to get back into huge debt like that. I sure don't!"

They both went quiet, and I saw a chance to get a word in edge-wise. "How did you get that number?"

"It was what we worked out based on some of those listings," replied Eleanor.

"Okay...and did you work out how much it would cost to renovate the home you already have?"

Both of them blinked. "We.... weren't sure of the total costs," replied Eleanor, who then chuckled. "I guess it's a good thing you're here, then!"

I laughed. "Indeed."

We got to work and after crunching the numbers, Tony and Eleanor were surprised to learn that borrowing $400,000 to invest in a renovation would cost them only $2,000 a month. Tom nodded his head slowly. "Now that is way more reasonable than buying a new house." He paused, then smiled. "Tell you want, I'll keep an open mind about the renovating, and I'll let you know." That was where matters stood as I left the house that day.

It took another month before Eleanor invited me back to their home. Tom opened the door and led the way to Eleanor seated at the kitchen table.

"Let's do it," she said, then turned her gaze to Tom. He was smiling and nodding.

I put the Agreement in front of them and they both signed without any hesitation on the dotted line. As Eleanor handed me the deposit cheque, she leaned in, and whispered, "Thank you so much, Gene. You can't imagine how long I've been waiting for this."

Oh yes, I can.

The Benefits of Staying Put

Eleanor's story is not unique. There's something to be said for loving where you live. Familiarity with the people, the parks, the local market, the excellent school, and even the secret traffic shortcuts: all go into the decision on whether to move or to stay put.

Unfortunately for most of us, the place we first settle into doesn't always serve us well over the long run once we buy a dog, start a family, or simply acquire more stuff. After all, needs change as the years go by. The space may feel tight, the furniture grows shabby, and the look runs stale. While some people are held back by sentimental feelings toward the house or the neighbourhood, others simply feel overwhelmed just by the thought of moving.

The result is that many homeowners, and particularly couples, will stay put longer than they should, turning a blind eye to the inadequacies of their surroundings until they just can't take it any longer. At some exasperating juncture, frustration wins over and the question "should we stay or should we go?" is given serious thought.

But let's face it: finding a house in Toronto and its surrounding areas that is less than $1 million these days is no easy feat. With such high prices, most people considering a move couldn't afford to buy back their own house at the current market price. So, if they're looking to upgrade, they're forced to head to the most far reaching suburban areas such as Orangeville, Barrie, or Kingston. An increasing number of buyers are choosing to commute two hours or more to and from Toronto just to get more housing bang for their buck.

The Hidden Costs of Moving

People often forget to consider the transaction costs of buying or selling a house. Let's break it down into dollars and cents (and sense). There are numerous fees and soft costs that come with buying a typical $2 million resale home in the Greater Toronto Area (yes, that's typical these days). The knowledgeable mortgage broker Gary Fooks provided me with approximate values for the soft costs buyers incur when they purchase a resale or a new built home (in the Toronto area in the year 2018). Here is a partial list of what goes into the purchase of a home:

A RESALE HOME

City of Toronto's Municipal Land Transfer Tax	$50,000
Ontario's Provincial Land Transfer Tax	$50,000
Realtor's commission payable on the home sold and home purchased	$150,000
Lawyer/appraisal fee	$10,000
Home inspection	$700
Moving expenses	$10,000
Drapery, landscaping, etc. (approx.)	$25,000
Catching up on deferred maintenance in the resale home both inside and outside including painting and roof shingles (approx.)	$50,000

TOTAL $350,000

The total soft costs are approximately $350,000, or about 20% of the selling price.

A NEW- BUILD HOME

In addition to all of the above costs, a typical new-build custom home
of $2 million in the GTA also has the following soft costs:

13% HST	$260,000
Development and education levies plus building permits fee as per the City of Toronto Building Department.	about $50,000
	TOTAL $650,000

Total soft costs are approximately, $650,000, or about 33% of the
selling price.

Even after spending all that money, it's not likely that you'll just
paint the walls and clean the carpets before moving in. In the case
of a resale, it's more likely you'll want some upgrades, such as a
new major appliance, updating the kitchen, or a new backyard deck.
Suddenly, you have a laundry list of soft costs that aren't adding value
in bricks and mortar. It's dead money that could be better spent on
an existing home through a partial or complete renovation. For many,
this is the tipping point.

No less important is the emotional aspect of relocating. It's not for the
faint of heart. In fact, some psychologists claim that only the death
of a family member, divorce, and the loss of a job are more stressful
than a home move.

Like Eleanor, many people prefer to renovate rather than move
because they like their neighbours, their community, and schools.
They also don't want to go through the disruption of moving or
running the risk of suffering the dreaded "buyer's remorse." There
is no guarantee they'll like the new place or the people. Staying put
allows the family to maintain stability and familiarity.

Naturally, there are a ton of variables when it comes to deciding whether to stay put and renovate or relocate to something with many of the bells and whistles already in place. We've all heard the horror stories: costs, months of dust and disruption in your home and life, unexpected problems and delays, budget overruns, poor-quality workmanship and unreliable contractors.

Canadians, however, have definitely caught the renovation bug. According to Statistics Canada data compiled by the real estate consultancy Altus Group Ltd., residential renovation spending (including alterations, improvements, conversions and repairs) across the country broke the $70-billion barrier in 2015.

Why renovate instead of move? Here's my assessment, based on years of experience in business:

Adds to the value when it comes time to sell and will increase your personal enjoyment for years to come.

Improves the comfort and functionality of the home as well as your lifestyle.

Additional space will accommodate the needs of your expanding family.

Updating and remodeling will transform your home into the trendy and glamorous appearance that you have been envisioning for years.

Mastering your makeover style will create a dream home that you can be proud of.

A functional and inviting living space brings the family together and creates a strong family unit.

Removing clutter and achieving a beautiful, functional and harmonious home reduces stress and, ultimately, makes the home a healthy, nurturing place.

Moving is one of the most stressful life experiences and contributes to hair loss, short-term memory problems and incredible anxiety.

There is a scarcity of new homes and resale in the GTA.

After 2018, the "move up" dreams of families have been squashed because they can't afford to buy as much now. More people are making their current home their forever home by renovating and making additions to it.

But that's just my opinion. Before you decide your next steps, do some honest soul searching by pondering all the reasons why you should honestly stay or go.

Making the Choice That's Right for You

Let's begin with the neighbourhood. Do you love it? And, I mean do you really love it? Consider all aspects: the people, the schools, the shops, the community centre and library, the trees (or lack thereof), the parks, the walkability score, the religious institutions, the traffic, and any other conveniences that have their place in your daily life. If you moved, how much would you miss those things? Remember, you can fix a house, but you can't replace an entire neighbourhood.

Next, think about your ultimate goals. Do you want more room or more rooms? People often decide to move because they crave extra space, but it's not always about adding square footage. A renovation that incorporates a creative layout can make the space more efficient; sometimes, all it takes is an addition of just one more room!

Even if the house doesn't become physically bigger, a little ingenuity can go a long way toward making a house feel more spacious. For example, a spacious three-bedroom home can be reconfigured to four bedrooms and allow a family to have a more efficient layout. An attached garage can be made into a bedroom, den or office with its own ensuite bathroom. Knock down the walls in a hall linen closet for a bigger washroom. Improve the flow and family vibe by removing walls between the kitchen and the family room for an open-concept design. Finishing the basement provides bonus space for the family without having to build an addition.

The attic, too, is a square-footage gold mine, especially in older homes with pitched roofs. Build stairs through the closet, add insulation and heating ducts … et voilà! You'll be shocked by the amount of usable space you never knew you had.

Consider what I call "the patience factor". This virtue is a necessity during renovations. It's a long-term commitment of time and energy, so only serious homeowners need apply. There will be countless decisions to make throughout the process, from cabinet door handles and paint colours to window coverings and landscaping. Patience (and interest) is required to set everything in place. Kitchens can take several months, new ductwork and wiring even longer. And since most timelines are based on estimates, how will you manage when the work isn't finished by the promised date? Are you even-keeled enough to handle it, or will you ride an emotional rollercoaster as plans unravel, tradesmen don't show up on schedule, and the dining room set doesn't arrive in time for your in-law's 50th anniversary party?

Be realistic about cost. Renovating is more than paying the contractor. Be sure to consider costs associated with architect plans, appliances, furniture, moving to temporary digs while under construction, an interior designer, and much more. It all adds up … and usually ends up costing more than estimated, so be sure to build extra cash into the budget. There's also the long-range picture to consider: will the renovation yield a higher selling price if you decide to sell at some point in the future? What's the eventual return on investment?

As for Eleanor and Tom, they had a terrific space to work with and they loved their neighbourhood, so why pack it in and start again?

They simply needed the confidence to turn their existing home into their Forever Home. And now, guests are regularly wowed by the transformation... and guess whose business card they keep asking for?

Questions to consider

o Why would you love to stay in your neighbourhood?

o Why would you love to remain in your home?

o What would you like to change about your home to make it your forever home?

Chapter 4

Love Where You Live

"A dream is a wish your heart makes."

– Disney's Cinderella

A Tale of Three Sisters

I received a call from Joan, a friend I've known since grade school, to come by her home to discuss renovations. Joan is the youngest of three sisters. As next door neighbours, we were always hanging out at each other's houses. Today, Joan lives in a prestigious area of southeast Oakville, an upper crust neighbourhood known for its top-notch private schools, chichi restaurants, and opulent homes.

When I arrived, I was surprised to be greeted by her two older sisters who were joining us. The three of them were sitting around the kitchen table chatting over tea and cupcakes.

I noticed Stacey, the eldest, first. I had never felt comfortable around her. I remembered her as a high achiever and perfectionist who had always strived for approval and acceptance from her parents. When we were young, Stacey was known for dominating conversations and draining the energy from those she lectured, especially her younger sisters. I'd heard that she'd become a successful pharmacist.

My immediate impression was that Stacey hadn't changed a bit! Dressed in a baggy tracksuit and baseball cap, she was aloof and cool, not even attempting to smile as I extended my hand. A chill went through my body as I shook her hand and recalled the night when I was 10 years old and Stacey had caught me picking apples from their backyard tree and then telling my father. I'd been grounded for a week because of it.

Joan's middle sister, Barb, greeted me warmly with a big hug. She was dressed in a pretty flowered skirt and light blue blouse with her dark hair tied back in a ponytail.

"Great to see you again, Gene!" she said, putting me at ease. She was always the nicer one. She'd even baked me an apple pie a few weeks after the backyard fiasco to cheer me up.

I remembered Barb as the perennial peacemaker, always concerned with what was fair and just for everyone. Today, she works as an IT consultant at Rogers, and not surprisingly, is the union steward there. She spends a lot of time with her co-workers and even plays on the company's women's hockey team. Joan had confided in me that this circle of friends was like family to her, perhaps even more so than her sisters.

Joan, the baby sister, always had a charming, bubbly personality that naturally drew people to her. She had a wide circle of friends and was now a successful entrepreneur running a medical spa business.

As the youngest, Joan had learned the importance of fending for herself. She claimed this was because her parents had always been too preoccupied with the older two to give her much attention. Although her parents had paid for her sisters' ballet and dance lessons when they were young, and later covered their university costs, by the time Joan finished high school, the parents' fund had apparently dried up. Joan was forced to apply for a student loan and proceeded to work two jobs to pay back the money.

She used to joke that she was the Cinderella of the family. Her sisters always laughed it off, but they all knew there was some truth to this. This work ethic that Joan was forced to develop paved the way for her future success, as well as her eventual rise up the social ladder.

After serving me tea, Joan delved into her renovation plans that included the addition of an enclosed Muskoka room off the kitchen, a finished basement with a theatre room and a larger master bedroom on the second floor with a huge walk-in closet and dressing room.

Before I had a chance to respond, Stacey chimed in.

"Why are you thinking of changing your house?" she asked. "It's only fifteen years old, and it looks great. Dad would turn in his grave if he knew you were wasting money on such a frivolous thing."

I bit my tongue as I recalled their father. He'd been in the Royal Air

Force and served in the Second World War. He was grateful to simply own a house when he came to Canada. Like many of his generation, he espoused the ideals of frugality and saving for a rainy day.

"Really? Look what happened to him," retorted Joan. "He saved all his money for retirement and never got to enjoy any of it by dying at the age of 55. I'm not going to live my life that way."

Stacey, it turned out, agreed with her parents' values. She was frugal with her money and had married a police officer who shared her beliefs. They had bought his grandmother's bungalow in Port Perry, and never invested a dollar into it. Content with a simple life, they'd saved virtually all their money. Their goal is to retire early and live off of their pensions.

Barb weighed in next. "I'm not really keen on renos. I had a bad experience with a home update a few years back. It was the mother of all money pits!"

"Oh?" I said. "What happened?"

"Well, my second husband and I had bought an older subdivision home on an Oakville golf course. Just loved the area at first sight! Right near the hockey arena where I played and everything! Thing was, we were only able to afford it because our in-laws had bought it for us. It was way bigger than our first home."

I nodded. "Sounds like it was lovely!"

"It was," said Barb. "So, after five years, my teenaged kids wanted more space to entertain their friends. I decided to finish the basement and, while we were at it, opening up the kitchen to the family room and dining room. You know, go more open concept."

Barb took a breath, and smiled sheepishly. "I admit it, we made every mistake in the book. I'd gotten two quotes, one at $175,000 and another at $120,000. I was just floored: those seemed super high to me! One night not long after that, I was having post-game drinks at my team's local bar. I told my teammates about the high quotes, and one of them referred me to a contractor named Jeff. 'He's very reasonable!' my friend said, so naturally, I arranged a meeting for the following weekend."

Uh oh, I thought. I can see where this is going.

"Jeff was pleasant said he could start the project right away. And it was only $90,000! I signed off on his estimate immediately. Afterwards, Jeff asked me for a $30,000 down payment so he could order the new kitchen. This seemed fair, so I paid him. We moved in with my in-laws when the demolition started."

Barb sighed again. "The project was only supposed to take three months, Gene," she said. "I hate to admit it but we were naive to the point of being stupid. The job stood still for six weeks after demolition without any progress. I kept calling Jeff but he didn't return my calls for days. And things just went from bad to worse. I ended up firing him, and lost my $30,000 deposit."

I nodded. I'd heard similar scenarios many times.

The Emotional Connection to Our Homes

Three sisters with three different attitudes towards their homes. There's Stacey the minimalist, Barb the pragmatist, and Joan, who believes in indulging in the fruits of one's labour. Joan is perfectly comfortable in a luxury home and belonging to the social circles of her wealthy neighbourhood.

Interestingly, all three sisters decided to own a home rather than rent. About two-thirds of Canadian families own their own home, which ranks near the top percentile in the world. But what is the motivation behind home ownership? Studies reveal that our motivations are driven by primal, instinctual needs as human beings. Understanding these needs uncovers why each of us has different attitudes towards our homes and what prompts our desire to improve them.

As I drove home from Joan's house that night, I started thinking about the emotional connections each of the sisters had to their own home. And then it hit me: Maslow's pyramid! Back in university, I'd taken a psychology course that had focused on just that.

American psychologist Abraham Maslow wrote a paper in 1943 entitled *A Theory of Human Motivation* in which he established a hierarchy of human needs. He developed a pyramid to describe the different levels. At the base level are basic physiological needs: air, food, drink, shelter, sleep. These are the first things that motivate our behavior. Once these needs are satisfied, the next level up fulfills the need for safety and security. This is proceeded by the desire to meet our psychological needs. They include qualities such as friendship, love, belonging, accomplishment, self-esteem, status and mastery. At the pinnacle of the pyramid is the desire to achieve our full potential, seeking personal growth and peak experiences.

In Maslow's view, human actions are based on goal attainment. Our needs follow each other in succession based on priority. Once the first level is fulfilled, he hypothesized, the next level up is what motivates us, and so on.

Here's how Maslow describes it:

"It is quite true that man lives by bread alone – when there is no bread. But what happens to man's desires when there is plenty of bread and when his belly is chronically filled? At once other (and "higher") needs emerge and these, rather than physiological hungers, dominate the organism. And when these in turn are satisfied, again new (and still "higher") needs emerge and so on. This is what we mean by saying that the basic human needs are organized into a hierarchy of relative prepotency."
(Maslow, *A Theory of Human Motivation*, p. 375).

As I understand it, this five-step theory is that once we satisfy our initial needs, we move up the pyramid to the next level in pursuit of self-actualization. Only when the lower-tier needs of physical and emotional well-being are satisfied can we begin to address the higher-order needs of influence and personal development. Conversely, if the things that satisfy our lower-order needs are swept away, we are no longer concerned about the maintenance of our higher-order needs.

Because this pyramid can be so widely applied to explain human behaviour, it has become a required study at many business schools and in psychology courses. I thought it made sense to apply this approach to help understand why women renovate their homes so differently and how they make an emotional connection to their homes. The relationship between how women renovate and Maslow's hierarchy of needs became more apparent once I started hosting focus groups and visiting hundreds of women in their homes to discuss their renovation ideas. I learned many interesting things along the way, particularly that when a woman improves her home base, she is making a statement. She's fulfilling her own physiological needs and desires.

Using Maslow's pyramid as a guide, a home can satisfy our needs on the first three levels. It's where we put down roots. It's where we can be ourselves, express ourselves freely, and spend meaningful time with family and friends to build relationships and family memories.

Safety in the Home

A home satisfies the need for shelter, safety, security, and protection against the elements. While a home protects from the cold and provides a hearth for warmth, I've seen many inherent dangers in peoples' homes that can threaten their physical safety and health. Damp conditions foster mold growth, which increases the risk of respiratory allergy symptoms and exacerbates asthma. In severe cases, mold can cause anaphylactic shock.

Mold can grow on and behind walls, in showers, in ceilings or in kitchen cabinets where water damage has occurred. Moisture problems can result from cracks or leaks in foundation walls, plumbing leaks, inadequate exhaust, flooding or roof leaks. Once you fix the cause of the moisture build-up in your home and remove the mold, you can breathe easy.

Another safety concern is knob-and-tube wiring. It was all the rage once upon a time, but it's oh-so-dangerous today! If your home was built before the 1940s and never updated or renovated, chances are good that you've got it. This type of wiring doesn't have a third wire for grounding, so it can't handle the power requirements of today's modern appliances, home technology, steam showers, hot tubs, pool filters, air compressors, in-floor heating, and other electricity guzzlers. It's unsafe and antiquated.

I've heard of way too many house fires attributed to DIY electricians (read: not experienced!) trying to help homeowners make the switch. If you're considering updating your wiring – which you should, even if you're not ready to renovate – be sure to hire a licensed electrician to do the job properly. It can be a matter of life and death!

One more silent killer is carbon monoxide poisoning caused by malfunctioning gas-burning appliances such as furnaces, ranges, water heaters, and room heaters. The only way to protect yourself is to install adequate exhaust and a carbon monoxide detector on every floor. Do it!

A Sense of Belonging

Now, let's say you fix the basic shelter, safety, and security needs. What's next? According to Maslow, it's all about "belongingness and love." When you consider the emotional connection many of us feel toward our homes, you can clearly see how Maslow's pyramid figures in to a homeowner's needs. The home is a source of comfort and a soothing environment for ourselves and our family. It is also a way to maintain loving relationships with family members.

Many people consider their home to be an extension of themselves. Women, especially, tend to make an emotional connection to their home by optimizing or remodeling it to make it more beautiful. They like to change the space by updating and adding to it so that it closely resembles their sense of "Home Sweet Home." When a woman returns home after a day at work or doing errands, she wants to feel delight and contentment. As the saying goes, home is where the heart is. The quest to create the perfect retreat fuels the need to renovate and remodel a home that doesn't live up to that vision.

Now, where does esteem fit in? On Maslow's pyramid, this encompasses anything that boosts our confidence, including recognition, attention, social status, accomplishment, and self respect. From a homeowner perspective, this relates to status. For many people, a bigger and better home is one more notch of accomplishment as they move up the social ladder.

The clothing you wear says a lot about you, as does the car you drive and even what you do for a living. The same goes for your dwelling. Your home makes a statement and says a lot about you. For most of the women I've met throughout my years as a builder and contractor, a renovation – whether big or small – is an opportunity for self-expression. A unique home environment to show off to family and friends puts a feather in her cap and raises her self-esteem. It reflects social and financial status. It builds self-esteem as she works her way up Maslow's pyramid.

Self-Actualization

Maslow describes the good life as one directed toward self-actualization. In his definition, it's the pinnacle need where we maximize our potential and do the best that we are capable of doing. Self-actualized people, he says, are motivated by truth, justice, wisdom, meaning and, interestingly, art appreciation. They have frequent peak experiences, which he defines as energized moments of profound happiness and harmony. However, only a small percentage of people reach this level.

Curiosity motivates women in particular to explore, to develop a better understanding of their environment and how to relate to it, and to acquire knowledge and wisdom. This is when women develop an appreciation for beauty and symmetry and a desire to reach their potential. Spiritual nature becomes important as they look beyond themselves and their own egos. Through self-actualization, they get a sense of wholeness and fulfillment as human beings.

Transfer that to the home analogy. When your home speaks to you on a deeper level – like a romantic partner, perhaps! – then making it your forever home makes sense. Your new improved home will feed your soul. That, in itself, is priceless. You will be more grounded when the magic and spirit of your remodeled home is in your life. A well-loved home nurtures you and can be your sanctum.

Joan and her sisters all had emotional connections to their homes, but each woman had a completely different attitude that can be related back Maslow's pyramid.

Stacey prioritized her need for safety and security. Because she thrives on structure, order and routine in her life, she chose a home in a safe neighbourhood and structured her life so she'd have financial stability. She achieved her emotional needs through the purchase of a house, thus resolving her fears and anxieties about being homeless and using the house as a financial instrument to fund her retirement. It makes sense that she doesn't care much about getting her emotional needs met by improving her house. She's a minimalist in life and in home décor. And she's happy that way.

Barb never had to strive to obtain the basics in life because her family took care of that. She sought out relationships and acceptance and yearned for a sense of belonging and community. It makes sense that she chose to live in a golf club community, where she could put down roots and easily interact with her work colleagues and neighbourhood friends. The highlight of her week is Sunday brunch at the golf course, not so much to eat but for the socializing. Naturally, her connection to her home comes from her need to create a cocoon with her family and friends. Barb is pragmatic and practical in her vision of creating her own Home Sweet Home.

Joan, the self-professed Cinderella of the family, grew up feeling that she was unloved. This compelled her to fill her self-esteem void. She sought respect from other people and worked feverishly to build her personal identity and reputation. Today she has achieved status, recognition, reputation, and appreciation, and still strives to boost her confidence through achievements.

It's no surprise then, that Joan wants to wow her family and friends by including all the latest trends and designs in her renovation. She has a personal shopper who keeps her closet filled with designer outfits, purses, shoes and jewelry. She has hired me and my company to do the work for her and design the most fashionable nest to impress her friends.

There is nothing wrong with that, Joan.
You've earned your glass slipper.

Questions to consider

○ What does your home say about you?

○ What do you want your home to say about you?

○ How does your home make you feel when you come home?

47

Chapter 5

Renovation Therapy, Anyone?

"Love hurts, love scars
Love wounds and mars
Any heart not tough
Or strong enough
Take a lot of pain

– Cher, Love hurts

'Till Renovation Do Us Part

"I wish you never would have started this project," screamed Daniela. "I'm too embarrassed to have anybody over to visit us!"

I shifted uncomfortably in my seat. The tension in the air was palpable. I was glad that we were doing this in their home and not a busy restaurant (although, if Jerry Maguire taught us anything, having people around might have stopped Daniela and John from making the very scene that was happening right in front of me).

We were in the family room of their Tudor-style home in North York. Daniela and John had bought it shortly after getting married, 14 years earlier. As it turned out, the place needed work, and John had promised to renovate the home himself. 14 years and three children later, it still wasn't done.

In fact, from where I was seated between the two of them (this must be what being a marriage counsellor feel like!), I could clearly see the plastic curtain hanging over the doorway to the kitchen. The family room had only recently been finished as part of the original repairs (and, from what I could see, John's handiwork was good, but not professional).

He and Daniela had opposite personalities, from what I observed. While Daniela was confident, outgoing, and spontaneous, John was a quiet homebody who preferred sticking to what he knew best. Based on my experience, these fundamental differences in personalities were at the root of their disagreements over renovation plans. John was extremely frugal, always trying to justify discretionary spending and worrying about household expenses and long-term savings. Daniela was more impulsive and preferred to spend now and worry later.

John made the decision to start their DYI project himself. As the renovation progressed, the decisions on design came fast and furious. Unfortunately, Daniela and John agreed on nothing. Visits to Home Depot turned into battles, both of them digging their heels into the ground when it came to the right colour of hardwood, the finish on the cabinets, backsplash tiles, even the hardware. Whatever frustrations the couple experienced before making the decision to renovate now paled in comparison to their current situation.

"I'm sick of living in a construction zone!" said Daniela, taking a sip of wine. "There's dust everywhere, all the time, and every time I get things just a little cleaned up and organized, you come around and decide to start the next phase."

John was clenching his jaw. His face was red, both from frustration and embarrassment. "I should never have made that promise," he said, "and I'm sorry, but honestly, honey, you're not helping. I'm working as fast as I can."

Before I could say something, Daniela leaned in again. "Yeah, well, you're not working fast enough."

"That's because I'm juggling two jobs and this project," replied John, his voice rising. "Time's a factor, too, you know."

"Don't I know it," said Daniela. "A year since this last 'phase' started, and it is nowhere near being done?"

"We haven't agreed on the colour of the floor tiles."

"That's because you're stubborn and you think you have better taste than I do."

"Oh yeah?" replied John, not even hiding his anger. "Maybe it's because you're a control freak who wants everything your way and doesn't want to listen to me, not even once!"

"Half the time, you're not even here to deal with the mess you've made! If you're not traveling or working in the basement, you're asleep on the couch because you're exhausted. Who do you think ends up having to take care of the kids?"

Daniela choked and sniffled, fighting back the tears that had started up. "You get to have a break. I've got to keep working and take care the kids while putting up with this mess that never stops. It's not fair!"

Daniela composed herself, cleared her throat, and looked at John, with complete honesty and hurt in her eyes. "Our family is suffering because you're an absentee father."

John sighed, put his face in his hands, then looked up at her "What do you want me to do? If I devote my nights and weekends to the renovation, you get mad at me because I'm not an attentive father. And if I spend time with you and the kids, you make snide remarks that I'm never going to finish the job. It's a no-win situation for me all I do is disappoint you."

Silence fell over the room, and finally I spoke up, trying to lighten the mood.

"Renovations are hard, aren't they?" I said.

Daniela and John both looked at me for a couple of seconds, then chuckled, breaking the tension in the air that, by that point, was thick enough to slather on toast.

"In retrospect," said John, "it was a huge mistake. This kind of project would be too time-consuming and stressful to tackle alone in this phase of our lives. I mean, the pressure from having children right away and my responsibilities as a software developer...I really should have seen that there was no way I could spend the time I needed swinging hammers and pounding nails."

"It wasn't like this when we met," said Daniela. "I was 20 years old and in university. I had such a huge crush on him. Not only was he adorably cute, with sandy blond hair and blue eyes, I fell in love with his kind heart, sense of humor, and strong work ethic. John was the perfect boyfriend. He made me feel special. We dated for two years and got married after graduation."

"You guys moved fast, then," I said.

"We did," said Daniela, pausing for a moment, and letting out a happy expression - the first time I'd seen her happy since I'd arrived. "As newlyweds, we were busy and happy. I loved being a nurse. John enjoyed his job as a software developer, and we both hoped to move into management. We enrolled in graduate school part-time. I eventually got a Masters degree in nursing administration, and John got a Masters in computer programming."

"So you were both very busy," I said. "That was before the kids came along, right?"

"I got pregnant soon after that" continued Daniela. "Although I planned to return to nursing after my maternity leave, I unexpectedly conceived Amanda when Samantha was just over a year old. Crunching the numbers, we realized it made more sense for me to stay home rather than work and pay for childcare. William came along three years later. That's when we started looking for a bigger house."

The mood was much lighter now, and I was able to see just how much strain these renovations had taken on what was otherwise a couple of very loving, affectionate, family-minded professionals in their own fields. "Why didn't you just hire contractors right off the bat, then?"

John, smiling now, gestured to Daniela to answer for him. "Unfortunately," she said, "during that time, the company John was working for lost their biggest contract and John was laid off. I was forced to go back to work as a hospital administrator. By the time John found a new job, house prices had escalated so much they were beyond our reach."

"Ah, I think I understand," I said. "You both seem to agree on the basics: you love this house, you want it to be a beautiful space for your family, and you just want it done. Really, where is the disconnect between you two?"

Daniela finished her wine and leaned in. "I'm really keen on just bringing in a good contractor to completely renovate the entire main floor, even add an addition out in the back." She nodded at John and sighed. "John is still squeamish about hiring a contractor because he believes it will be prohibitively expensive."

I turned to John, who also nodded. "I know I've been procrastinating, and I'm sorry for that, I really am. But I'm pretty handy with a hammer and nails myself. I know I can do a lot of the work myself. Plus, I'm good at multi-tasking. I got that from my father: he's was a DIY pro. This- " He gestured to the doorway to the kitchen and the family room, "was normal for me growing up. Pops always had different projects on the go at the same time."

Daniela sighed again, exasperated. "Your dad was an auto mechanic, dear. Those different projects weren't exactly happening in the living-room or kitchen. Plus, it's not a matter of if you can get it done, dear, it's when. I'm tired of waiting for the perfect time for you to finish." She turned to me. "I am exhausted waiting for my husband to finish what he started! I have spent months interviewing several contractors and after meeting you Gene, I know I've found who I want to go with. I'm anxious to sign an agreement and get this renovation finished."

"Yes," said John, "and you want to pay for it using an equity loan on the house. That just makes me nervous." I felt the tension starting to build again as he continued. "You're right: we should've sold the house before the market took off, but now I'm just in love with this community and..." He paused. "I guess...I'd just feel this tremendous sense of loss and defeat if we just left."

Daniela shook her head. "It's too late to think about what could have been. It's time to make this house more functional for our family." She turned to me. "Our marriage is suffering the longer he sits on his hands deciding whether we should move, renovate, hire or do it himself. I've...I've just had enough!"

Keeping the Peace

When I hear about a couple splitting up over "irreconcilable differences", it's really just code for "renovation-related issues".

All kidding aside (well, somewhat kidding), it's not unusual for couples to struggle through a renovation. While decorating or building a new home can certainly be fun and fulfilling, it is also frustrating and difficult. Renovating is a time-consuming, nerve-wracking, stressful experience that is bound to affect your personal life in one way or another.

From finances to design decisions, renovating can be very hard on a marriage or relationship. Fights over money and style can really take a toll. If a couple is not careful they might walk into divorce court before setting foot in their dream home. What's at the root of these disagreements?

Let's face it: most of us want to feel we are in control - if not all the time, then most of the time - so it's important to recognize from the onset of a renovation who is in control of what. Who controls the wallet? Who decorates the house? Who's going to make most of the financial and home decor decisions? Before the saws and hammers come out, it's best to have a discussion on who is leading the project.

In my experience, it's usually the woman. The truth is that most women are fiercely protective about how they want their homes to look. In my opinion, it's just one of those things that women intuitively know better.

Each relationship is different, so it's impossible to pinpoint exactly what may be the cause of renovation battles. However, over my years in this business, I've come to observe that relationships are more likely to weather the storm of a renovation when the men step to the sidelines.

While maintaining a voice in the plans and decisions is absolutely important, women are likely to prefer to take the lead in the design and décor. My advice for all you husbands out there? Let them.

This means the practical choice will not always be worth the fight. That's not to say that one partner simply bows out of the process altogether, either. A renovation can also be an opportunity for quality time together and date nights (at the hardware store).

So, what is it about renovation the causes mental stress? It's not too hard to understand when you think about it. Your quality of life is affected during the work; there's a feeling of lack of control, stress over finances (especially when unexpected challenges arise), and the big one: feeling like the project will never end.

Here are some key ingredients to achieving the goals for your renovation project so when you're done you will still have a happy relationship.

Identify Your Dreams and Plan Properly

It still amazes me how much couples argue and bicker over the tiniest of issues, from the kind of countertops to the choice of paint.

First, understand that both of you have the same overall idea about what the project will end up looking like, but you might have slight variations on precisely what that end product will actually be. You have to figure out how you want to feel in your home when all is done. How do you want to live? The key here is to listen to each other and don't judge! At this early stage, every idea is valid. You want to hash out as many decisions as possible before you swing a hammer.

Be sure you and your spouse are on the same page. Before you start, sort your styles, choices, and visions for the project. Don't even start the renovation project if you haven't done this. Trust me, if you can't decide on things upfront when it's calm, you certainly won't be able to during a screaming match when the clock is ticking, the workers are standing around, and the pressure is really on!

Let Go of Your Preconceived Notions

Construction is not going to be cheap, no matter how you swing it, and even the most frugal of homeowners are going to be seduced by the glamourized showrooms that make it easy to upgrade to that six-burner range or the newest Brazilian hardwood floor.

Both partners are going to have some concept of how much it will cost and how long it will take. Again, listen to each other. One thing I've noticed that many couples do is poke fun at their significant other whenever they raise an idea that seems ridiculous. Never laugh at your spouse. If you ridicule your partner, they will clam up and be that much less open to your desires when it's your turn to be heard.

It's normal for couples to not know the cost of renovation. This is especially understandable today when most of the exposure couples have had to home renovations are from reality TV shows that are simply unrealistic when it comes to costs and budgets ("Hi, I'm Mary, and this is my husband Bart. Bart is a professional mime, and I make a living from embroidering birds on couches. Our budget for this renovation is $40,000 dollars").

In fact, if you do get most of your information from entertainment, you should check out a great sleeper hit from the 1980s called The Money Pit, starring Tom Hanks. It will show you, with surprising realism for a comedy, everything that can go wrong with a renovation. At the very least, it'll show you just how much worse your situation could be!

The budget is the most common cause of argument among couples taking on a renovation. I suggest that you both sit down and make a list with three headings: must have, nice to have (if possible), and optional. Keep as many of your items under "Must Have" as you can, because that's why you're renovating in the first place.

Your "Nice to Have" list shouldn't have more than 10% to 25% of your changes, depending on your budget and financial ability.

Finally, when you've finished sorting your "Optional" items, throw all of them out! They're optional for a reason, and this exercise helps you tell them apart from the changes you really need.

Lastly, try and avoid a tight timeline. If you know ahead of time that someone's getting married, you have a long-planned trip to Europe or Asia that's already booked around the time of the main build the main build, or it's coming up on Christmas, factor all of these things into your timeline.

Trying to get it done too quickly will add stress that you don't need. Give yourself a lot of time.

Divide the Decision-Making Responsibilities

I recall one housewife telling me that she and her husband "work best together in separate rooms." There's quite a bit of wisdom behind that simple sentence.

Fighting over decision-making powers is pointless. Its best to always give in because no one wins the Renovation Game. However, you can decide, ahead of time, who's in charge of what.

Make a list of all the decisions to be made and divide up the decisions as homework. For example, let one partner choose the kitchen countertops while the other chooses the flooring. Working with a professional designer can help you integrate different ideas in to one concept. Agree to honor the advice and direction of the designer.

Ultimately, when done right, the finished project is going to be beautiful either way. It's not worth digging in your heels in over the choice of hardware. Let your partner have the freedom over his or her design choices.

Demolition is the Most Stressful Time

If you take nothing else away from this chapter, please let it be this. For your sanity, do not live in your home during construction. Dust will get everywhere, noise will be nonstop during the day, and strangers will constantly be in and out of your home.

You are going to face days and maybe even weeks without a kitchen, bathroom, or other facilities. On top of that, you'll find yourself making a lot of last-minute decisions as well as unexpected changes to your plans when the work doesn't go as expected. It's vital that you both stay on the same team, and you can't do that if you're living there while the work's getting done.

Budget for a night in a hotel or a weekend away halfway through the project. You know that B&B that you both keep talking about, but never seem to actually stay at? Remember that restaurant in New York you saw on TV that you couldn't wait to try? Demolition is the time to go!

Celebrate!

Without giving away any spoilers, The Money Pit really does have a happy ending: that moment when all the arguments melt away as you admire the finished project and what you accomplished together.

Even though it won't always seem like it during the work itself, there will come a time when the contractors have hammered in the last nail, have swept away all of the dust, and everything is done! The home that you dreamed about is now a reality!

As you achieve goals, break out the champagne. In fact, I'd suggest doing this not just when the project is done and you're having a housewarming party, but the small goals. Celebrate when the cabinetry is all done, when the floor tiles are dry, and when that new walk-in closet is finally installed.

Remember What's Important: Marriage and Your Family

Throughout the entire renovation, there are no design emergencies or decisions that are more important than your partner. If you see that they are digging in like it's World War I, chances are they feel like they're not being heard, or that they're being steamrolled by the decision making.

Take a deep breath and have a conversation with them. Listen to what they have to say and do your best to alleviate their anxieties. Talk about keeping your eye on the prize, which is the completed project, the home that you both want.

And on the flipside, if you find that you're the one who needs to be heard, pick your battles. If it really doesn't matter to you whether the room is blue or yellow, let it go.

Most of all, remember that the three most important words in a marriage are "you're right, dear."

(And also mind the following six words: "If mama ain't happy, nobody's happy")

Do your best to stay lighthearted, don't take any of it too seriously, and remind yourself about the romance. What doesn't cause you to divorce during the project will give you a great story to laugh about for years to come. If you're still laughing at the end of the project, that's a good sign. You're going to be okay!

Here are my top tips for maneuvering a successful renovation:

- Communicate and listen to your partner

- When confronted with disputes, take a deep breath and compromise

- Divide the decision-making process so that one partner gets 51% and the final say

- Divide the responsibilities in such a way that one partner gets to run the design and decorating while the other manages the agreement negotiation

- Stay within the budget and agree to changes

- Polish your negotiating skills

- Take the stress out of the renovation with date nights

- Stock your liquor cabinet with lots of wine (that's a joke!)

Questions to consider:

- Do you and your partner have a shared vision for your home?

- Do you and your partner communicate well?

- Do you and your partner listen to each other?

Chapter 6

What Women Want

"Whatever makes me happy and sets you free"

–Christina Aguilera, What A Girl Wants

I get a kick out of people. Whether they're funny or quirky, peculiar or irritating, they always leave me with great story to tell. From decades of visiting families in their home this is one of my favorite stories.

My oldest son had arranged for me to meet with his hockey coach Bob at his Etobicoke home which backed onto the Markland Woods golf course.

I was greeted by their oldest son Ryan who played hockey with my son. "Good to see you, Mr. Maida," he said, "I'll take you into the family room". When we got there, his father, Bob, his mother, and sister were watching TV together. The credits were rolling on a movie that had just finished.

Bob got up to greet me. I could see right off the bat that Bob was a hockey guy, with a Maple Leafs jersey and golf hat.

"Nice to meet you!" said Bob, warmly shaking my hand. "Come on in! This is my wife Kathy." Kathy and I shook hands. In stark contrast to Bob, she was dressed in a fashionable blouse and skirt. Looking at both of them side by side, they reminded me of the Odd Couple.

"And this is Nancy, our daughter." Nancy stood up. "Nice to meet you, sorry about Mr. Leafs Nation here," she said, gesturing at Bob.

"That's okay," I said, "it's good to root for the home team."

"Yeah," said Nancy, "I'd just be happy if Dad would root for a winning team."

"Yeah, that's enough out of you," said Bob, chuckling. As we all sat down, I glanced at the TV.

"What were you guys just watching?"

Nancy and Kathy smiled at each other and spoke in near-unison. "What Women Want".

"Oh?" I said. "That's the one with Mel Gibson, right?"

For those of you who haven't seen What Women Want, in the film, Gibson plays Nick Marshall, a sleazy, chauvinistic Chicago advertising executive who is an ace at selling to men and seducing women. One day he slips and falls into his bathtub while holding a hairdryer and gets an electric shock. Upon waking up the next day, Nick realizes he can hear women's inner thoughts.

Soon Nick is "eavesdropping" on their minds and uses their ideas as inspiration for his own ad campaigns. In his quest to gain even more insight, makeup and waxing make for some pretty hilarious scenes.

I privately thought how much easier my business and life would be if I had Mel Gibson's power of knowing what women really want.

"Yeah, I guess," said Bob, "Mel Gibson was much better in Braveheart and Lethal Weapon."

"Oh, come on, Dad," said Nancy, "you didn't think Mel Gibson waxing his legs was funny? I couldn't stop laughing!".

"To be honest," I said, chiming in, "while I generally love Mel Gibson, one of my favorite movies is Tootsie, with Dustin Hoffman. Anyone ever see that?"

"No," said Nancy, "what's it about?"

"It's about an actor who's desperate to find work, so he disguises himself as a woman to land a female role. Hilarity ensues, as you can imagine."

"Sounds a bit like Mrs. Doubtfire!" said Nancy.

"Not quite the same, but kind of in the same genre", I said.

As Bob, Kathy and I sat down to talk, I started to think how many other actors played women in film and TV, having the chance to look at life through the eyes of a woman with a whole new perspective. Actors such as Tony Curtis and Jack Lemmon in Some Like it Hot, or, more recently, Tyler Perry as Madea Simmons in Diary of a Mad Black Woman.

And, as Nancy observed, who could forget Robin Williams' classic portrayal of Mrs. Doubtfire?

It was interesting, then, meeting with this particular couple, and noticing just how different their perspectives were. Bob was and is a classic Alpha male who is very comfortable in a hockey changeroom amongst chauvinistic men. Kathy, on the other hand, has a strong personality with a warm material side who is happiest being surrounded by family.

It's not that Bob didn't have a voice at all: it just seemed that he was very comfortable relinquishing his power to Kathy when it came to decorating the nest.

"We met in university," said Kathy, looking at her husband with obvious affection. "Bob was on the varsity hockey team. He was every bit the jock but was also really sweet."

"Yeah, he really was," said Bob, kissing Kathy's hand, then turning to me. "We hit it off, and after we graduated, we got married. I got a job as a hockey coach for the university, and Kath ended up becoming a CA for a large accounting firm."

As we talked, I quickly saw that they both had gone through four of the five stages of life:

Adolescence ✓   Kids ✓

Bachelorhood ✓   Renovation.

Marriage ✓

This last phase is where they couldn't agree.

"Honestly, Gene, no offence," said Bob, chuckling, "but renovating sucks. I've heard so many horror stories from my friends who've gone through renos and on the other side of it, they were just catatonic, not to mention bankrupt. Not something I want to get involved with, not ever."

"Do you like your home the way it is?" I asked him.

Bob nodded emphatically. "Yep, absolutely. Don't want to change a thing. Not going to. The most I'd do is make a man-cave for my hockey memorabilia and trophies."

I smiled and looked over at Kathy. "What do you think?"

Kathy sighed, clearly unhappy. "Well, there's no way I'd approve a man-cave. It would separate Bob from the rest of the family. I want to make sure that we have a family gathering space so we can all be together, and entertain together, like we're doing right now."

"So why are you considering renovating?" I asked.

"Well, after the kids were born, I made a lot of sacrifices to balance my work and home life. But time just flew by, years turned into decades, and the other day, I came home after a really tough day at the office and just found that everything was so messy and cluttered. Of course, who had to clean it up? It is like I am working two jobs."

Kathy leaned in closer. "But that was my a-ha moment. This is the time to make all the changes I want to make in the house. The place is really busting out at the seams in some areas. I'm sick of just stuffing everything I own in closets that are way too small for a growing family and the lifestyles that we're leading right now. Honestly, I've had enough with the chaos around here."

She sat back, took Bob's hand again. Bob, for his part, had gone quiet and, despite his never-gonna-renovate bluster only a couple of

67

minutes earlier, now seemed deferential and supportive.

"We're doing this, Gene. It's time."

There was no question who ruled the roost in this household.

Home Design Trends

If there's one thing I've learned from my three decades of interviewing families in their homes, it's that women do indeed rule the roost.
Gone are the days of the 1950s when Father knew best, most women
stayed home to raise children, and people lived frugally. Today,
women are major breadwinners and powerful corporate leaders. They
are strong role models, make the bulk of the family decisions, and
have tremendous spending power.

Almost everything about the modern home is created with women in
mind. In his book What Women Want (no relation to the Mel Gibson
movie), Paco Underhill explains that the days of the male-oriented
house are over. Instead, builders are accommodating the modern
lifestyle needs and demands of the strong female who runs the household. As Underhill writes: "The fact of the matter is that females have
elevated not just the contemporary kitchen but the bathroom into
places that both recognize and salute their status."

As women entered the workforce in greater numbers and families got
used to two incomes, they improved their standard of living. Conse-
quently, builders stepped on the gas. When two-car families became
the norm, two-car garages did, too. The Internet made it possible for
people to work from home, coining the term home office. And with
the advent of infomercials, The Shopping Channel, and eventually
online shopping, we acquired more stuff and craved more space.

It's no wonder that homes built a century ago – or even a few decades
ago – have passed their best-before date. Women have emerged as

the key decision-makers in home design and now have a lot of pull in what happens in the house. They're demanding homes that are livable, that reflect their personalities and lifestyles and that make their lives easier.

It's all about open-concept floor plans, great rooms, and extra bedrooms to accommodate nannies and aging parents. There's more natural light with wider windows and skylights. Kitchens are open to the family room and are the hub of the household, with large quartz islands and caeserstone countertops perfect for eating, entertaining and homework. Hands-free electronic faucets are the new must-have feature, as is the walk-in pantry complete with a whiteboard to jot down grocery lists. Whirlpool bathtubs are being replaced with spacious custom showers with niches for shampoo. Toilets conserve water, fans are humidity-controlled and "floating" vanities are all the rage.

Why schlep dirty clothes up and down the stairs? Position the washer and dryer upstairs near the bedrooms or in the master suite. Clothes can come out of the dryer and go straight into the bedroom closet. Then there's the "drop zone" that has so many women swooning. It's that area between the garage and the kitchen, comprising of shelves, cabinets, a bench to take off shoes, a mail slot, even lockers for jackets. Backpacks, shoes, keys, cell phones, briefcases and the like can be dumped in one place, meaning a lot less hunting for stuff in the mornings and less clutter spilling into the kitchen. Simple, but super convenient!

And let's not forget all the new energy-efficient features, safety features and time-saving conveniences. Only the best will do when it comes to LED lighting, programmable thermostats and smart home technology. Fire alarms, smoke detectors, carbon monoxide detectors and moisture detectors work in tandem to keep the home safe. Smart home security systems have cameras and let you turn off the lights and furnace from your smartphone even when you're not home.

By the way, with all this attention to detail, why leave home in the first place? It's no wonder people are travelling less and cocooning more. With Netflix, Apple TV and incredible home theatres, who needs to go to the movies? With exquisitely landscaped backyards featuring pools and basketball courts, as well as awesome basements and exercise rooms, why join a gym? With wine fridges, steam ovens and barbecues, why go out to eat when you can entertain at home in style in your private oasis? And with a dog bath in the mudroom, even Spot wants to stay indoors!

In my honest opinion, there's no reason to keep living in a ticky-tacky home just for the sake of a few memories. Times have changed. Get with the program!

Homes have traditionally been designed by men. This has caused a huge disconnect over the years when it comes to the finished product. Organization and storage have been lacking, finishes haven't been up to snuff, rooms have been small or closed off. Yet women directly purchase or have controlling influence in the purchase of more than 90% of all renovation and home makeovers.

Because women are the decision-makers and differ in their renovation decision process, men should design homes based on what woman want. That means sensible designs that appeal to both a woman's sensitivities and practical needs.

Among the most essential features that meet this goal are:

Larger-than-average laundry room - The laundry room is the command centre and hub of activity in a modern household. With time at a premium, many families are doubling the volume of clothing they launder and are doing it in a room that can better accommodate it. Think two-washer/dryer machine sets, built-in ironing boards, floor-to-ceiling cabinets with compartments for everything, a clothes drying rack and even a dog-grooming shower pan with its own spray nozzle and drain.

Family locker room - Goodbye mudroom, hello stylish family locker room where even guests enter the house! This organized front or rear passageway is a home's first "Wow!" thanks to exquisite cabinetry, porcelain floors and artwork.

Modern butler's pantry - Not just for storage, the pantry now features separate space where food preparation can be hidden from guests. Similar to a work kitchen, it often accommodates additional counter space, cold drawers and cooktops/built-in ovens.

Ensuite spa - Women have elevated the bathroom to a place that recognizes and salutes their "All About Me" status. It's gone from a little dark room to a rain forest with only a hint of a toilet. Free-standing vessel tubs offer up a luxurious and relaxing atmosphere, though many homeowners are eschewing the tub for something equally zen-like to get them out the door sooner: extra-wide shower spray jets, a roomy area for steam, tons of storage space and even a quiet nook for reading. It's all the conveniences of hotel living in the comfort of your home.

Cool ceilings - Ceiling design can easily adapt to most styles, from traditional to transitional to contemporary. With artisanal plaster work a dying art, modern materials such as wood, plastic and high-strength resins are moving in. Vaulted ceilings with indirect lighting, sloped or cathedral ceilings provide architectural definition and add visual interest to a room. Coffered ceilings with detailed work that feature contrasting colours make any room seem warm, elegant and high-end.

Dressing room - Dressing rooms need to have ample natural light and space to create a comfortable experience. Pull-out valet poles allow for planning outfits and storage of dry-cleaning. Full length mirrors are a must, along with steam hangers and hide-away ironing board. Convenient storage for luggage and a pull-out waist height counter to rest open suitcases creates easy packing for jet setters or those who travel extensively for business.

Closet - The closet is about so much more than just a space to store clothes. It is an extension of a woman's self and a way of showcasing her personal style. Here, she will store her most precious belongings, and those things that beautify her and make her feel glamorous. Lighting is important to showcase her wardrobe. Shoe storage for pumps, boots and flats will take centre stage. Wall to wall shelving that is full height is a must. Clear divider drawers for sunglasses, bracelets, gloves and scarves makes finding accessories a snap.

Gene's Top 10 list of What Women Want in a Home

10. Experience – Women filter home plans through the lens of "How does this home live?"

9. Room for Stuff – Women evaluate home design based on storage. Families accumulate a lifetime of stuff and women insist on abundant storage where it's needed. That means in the kitchen, pantry, linen closet, laundry room, bathrooms, and closets.

8. Sociability – Women embrace others, so they look for spaces in their homes suitable for entertaining formally and informally. Today's lifestyle makes the kitchen the primary entertaining area. Most women would rather have a bigger kitchen than a bigger master bathroom. Blended families thrive with separate common areas and private areas. Modern families want rooms for media-related get-togethers.

7. Multi-tasking – Woman want designs that complement meaningful activities such as a home office, meetings, gourmet cooking, entertaining and homework stations.

6. Flexibility – Women care about their ever-changing families so they look for flexible designs to meet their current and future needs such as caring for aging parents, running a home-based business, space for their visiting adult children and grandchildren, his-and-hers offices, music rooms, craft rooms, offices that can be become dining rooms and dens that can become bedrooms.

5. Chill Time – Women create areas to de-stress, relax, and recharge. They look for serene spaces such as soaking tubs, walk-in showers, cozy spaces to curl up and read, meditate, do yoga, and connect on social media. They want low-maintenance areas so they don't become a slave to their own home.

4. Organization – Women insist on ways to help organize their homes: drop zones for mail or keys, closet systems, shoe racks. They want bigger kitchen pantries because they are cooking less but not eating less. They want more storage for prepared foods and appliances.

3. Fun – Women appreciate the element of surprise through unexpected design aspects.

2. Fashion – Women value fashionable designs through multiple style choices and various finish selections.

And the #1 thing that women want in a home renovation?

1. The Wow Factor – They crave validation, but they want a "Wow!" that makes sense through sophisticated, unique, practical designs that make a statement.

In short, women want respect from their home renovation. They want to feel secure. They want to be wowed. They want to find time for themselves while celebrating their uniqueness. And if they can have fun while doing it, all the power to them!

Questions to consider:

o Is there enough storage space in your home?

o Is there room to entertain and have family gatherings?

o Do you have your own private space to relax?

Chapter 7

Happy Home, Happy Life

"When I was five years old, my mother always told me that happiness was the key to life. When I went to school, they asked me what I wanted to be when I grew up, I wrote down "Happy." They told me I didn't understand the assignment, and I told them they didn't understand life."

– John Lennon

Limiting Beliefs

There's something about kitchens that make people spill the (coffee) beans.

Two years ago, I was sitting with a couple in their kitchen in Bloor West Village on a sunny morning. Karen was an X-ray technician at the local hospital and her husband, Frank, was a Crown attorney. They lived in a typical two-storey home for that area, with the garage at the back of the house off of a shared laneway.

Karen wanted to build a three-storey addition with a basement walkout, a new larger kitchen, and a new master bedroom with an ensuite and walk-in closet. She told me her budget for the project was $300,000.

Before we signed our Agreement, we did our investigation and found many existing problems with the house: the electrical system was not up to code, there was mold in the walls that had to be removed, and there was an old oil tank buried in the rear yard where the addition's new foundation would be going. Price tag: about $200,000 extra, (and that was before we even started the renovation)!

Naturally, Karen wasn't too pleased with this unexpected news and I could see her eyes start to well up. So I turned to Frank and, as I often do (but shouldn't), blurted out what was on my mind:

"How did you plan to pay for all this, Frank?"

"Well," said Frank, "Karen had inherited about $300,000 from her aunt. She wanted to use it to create her dream home. She had told all the nurses at the hospital about her exciting new project and they'd all been so happy and encouraging. Now, with the added costs that we hadn't counted on, it seemed that our dream might not come true at all. Karen was just devastated."

I felt terrible hearing that. Still, those upgrades had to be done before we could start any new construction. So, using my best Robin Hood voice, I offered to help them. "That's just awful. If you want, I can arrange some financing for the additional costs."

"No," replied Karen, almost right away. "That's out of the question."

Frank looked at her but said nothing.

"What about increasing your mortgage?" I asked. "Lots of my customers do that." She looked at me, horrified.

"I don't have a mortgage!" she practically bellowed, her face turning a deep shade of red. "Seriously, Gene, we can't afford to spend more! We have a budget! Nobody's planning to die and leave us more money any time soon! This is it! What part don't you understand?"

Whoa! That came out of left field. Yes, she was pretty anxious and upset. And yes, perhaps I should have let them talk about the financing alone instead of opening my big mouth right then and there. But alas, it was too late to take anything back. So, taking a couple of deep breaths, I plodded ahead.

"Karen," I said slowly and, I hoped, reassuringly, "most of our customers finance the equity in their home to fund their projects. They borrow the money they need to get their needs met. You and Frank can, too."

"Nope, I can't do that," she said.

"Why not?"

"I'm not that kind of person, Gene. I wasn't brought up that way. We used our wedding money for the down payment on the house and my parents gave us the rest of the money for the other half as a gift. We never had a mortgage and we're certainly not going to start at this stage in our lives."

Finally, Frank piped up. "Okay, now you've done it, Gene," he said, rolling his eyes ever so slightly as a smile parted his lips. "Get ready for the farm story!"

Karen shot him a look, then turned back to me. "My mother taught me never to get too big for my britches," she said. "I grew up on a dairy farm in Guelph. We were so frugal that there was always some kind of crisis at home. If the price of milk changed just a little bit, my parents' moods would just go from bad to worse. Dad was always worried that we'd lose the house."

"Okay," I said, "but what does that have to do with borrowing money?"

"Mom always said that banks wanted to loan you money so they can profit by taking your house when you're late with your payments. I know now that's not exactly accurate, but I do know that being in debt to the bank is never a good thing. We never had a mortgage and I don't want to take risks."

I chewed on that for a few quick seconds before turning to Frank. "How does it sit with you, Frank? How do you feel about Karen's decision? Do you think anyone will ridicule her for spending money on her own home? Is living mortgage-free the only way to feel safe?"

I didn't wait for him to answer and quickly turned back to Karen. "Karen, your home has doubled in value in the past ten years and you've built up over a million dollars in equity. It's a fabulous location. It's two blocks from the subway and a ten-minute walk from the lake. If you borrowed $200,000, the monthly payment would only be $1,000 per month. That's $33 a day!"

They stared at each other. I couldn't stop myself, as usual. (And hey, I was on a roll).

"Have you ever heard of limiting beliefs? That's what you've got, Karen.

I have a confession to make. I had limiting beliefs, when I was a kid. I didn't think I was good enough. I didn't have confidence. I always kept my mouth shut. I only found my voice after attending the seminar "Unleash Your Power" by Tony Robbins where I learned the skills to break through my disempowering beliefs. And after I successfully walked on hot coals, while attending the seminar, I realized I had the power to face my fears and overcome them. I now know that it's okay to speak up, so I'm going to do that now because I can see how much you want this addition. Your finances are none of my business, but renovation is my business. You've got two incomes that could more than handle the loan. Just saying!"

I paused for a moment, and realized that there was nothing left for me to say here. "Take your time and think about it and let me know what you decide."

A few weeks later, Karen called me. She'd thought about it a lot. She'd spoken to Frank. She'd gone to see the bank manager. And after making a list of all the pros and cons, she finally agreed that it made financial sense to get a loan and make her dream come true. As Frank told me later, she decided to stop listening to the voices in her head that caused her fear, and rather let her happiness take precedence.

"I owe you one, Gene!" he said. "It's taken her years to realize that she's an adult now and not under her parents' roof. She can make her own decisions without the fear of being judged by them. What a breakthrough! If renovation doesn't work out for you, Gene, buy a couch and become a psychologist!"

Ha!

I give credit to Tony Robbins for helping me see the situation for what it was: a classic case of unconscious programming. Karen's need to be happy in her own beautiful home proved stronger than her outdated beliefs and fears about borrowing money.

Eventually, Karen did make an appointment with her bank manager and had no trouble securing the loan. When we signed the renovation agreement, she couldn't stop smiling.

Six months after the renovation was completed, Karen invited me over for Easter brunch. The place looked amazing. What a transformation! There was no doubt that Karen was thrilled with the result. The home lifted her spirits. Everyone indulged her bragging rights at work. She felt so much more relaxed and slept better at night. She couldn't get enough of entertaining.

But the best part? Guess who was also invited for brunch? Her parents! I stayed in the kitchen to chat with Karen and her mom as they cleared the dishes and arranged dessert. I winced as the conversation turned to financing the home renovation. How awkward would this get?

"The house is just so beautiful, Gene," her mom said as she looked at me. "Must have cost a bundle?" I opened my mouth to speak, but Karen beat me to it.

"Worth every penny, mom," Karen gushed. "I can't believe I almost didn't do it!" I looked for the quickest exit, just in case this conversation heated up (you know what they say, if you can't take the heat, get out of the kitchen, literally).

"Really?" her mom asked, eyes wide. "I honestly didn't know how you were managing to live in this house. I didn't ever want to tell you because I didn't want to upset you, but this house has been in need of a major overhaul for a while."

Karen's mouth dropped open as her gaze moved from her mother to me, and back to her mother.

"Pardon?" she asked. "Do you know we had to borrow money to do this?"

Her mother beamed. "Well, that doesn't surprise me. Look at how beautiful your home is now. A total transformation!"

Before I knew it, I blurted out "so, you're not totally against the whole idea of mortgages?" (Oops. Where was that quick escape again?)

She laughed. "Of course not. Karen has been very fortunate to have never carried a mortgage, but that's not reality for most people. Right, honey?"

She turned to her daughter. "Aren't interest rates low right now, too?"

Karen, however, was too dumbfounded to respond.

I thought about a quote from Tony Robbins that I just love: "The only thing that's keeping you from getting what you want is the story you keep telling yourself." I had a feeling Karen was learning that lesson right now.

Defining Your Happiness

I can't tell you how many times I've heard women take a big sigh and say, "I just want to be happy."

What exactly does that mean? What, exactly, is this thing called "happiness?" It's important to know the definition because it's hard for your wishes to come true if you aren't clear on what your particular state of happiness looks like.

In my view, the best place to start defining happiness is by clarifying what it is not. Many people believe that happiness is the satisfaction of a fine meal, having fun at a party, enjoying a new adventure, the thrill and passion of sex ... you get my drift. These are all wonderful experiences to be cherished and cultivated. But in my view, they are not "happiness."

The way I see it, these experiences are the definition of "pleasure." They are experiences that you have and then they pass: a meal to savour and then digest, a party to enjoy and then let wind down, a passion to delight in followed by the warm afterglow to linger in. Pleasure is fleeting. Chasing pleasure is not happiness.

If happiness is not the same thing as pleasure, then what is happiness?

Happiness is when your life fulfils your needs. It arrives when you feel satisfied and fulfilled. Happiness is a feeling of contentment, that life is just as it should be. Perfect happiness – or, as some like to call it, enlightenment – comes when you have all of your needs satisfied.

Renowned life coach Tony Robbins gets it. Together with psychologist Cloé Madanes, he has revolutionized the field of life coaching and human needs psychology. In her book "Relationship Breakthrough" Cloé explains the key to happiness.

According to Tony and Cloé, human beings can only achieve success and happiness if certain fundamental needs are met. Through his work with millions of people all over the world, he's come to understand that human beings are motivated by the desire to fulfil six core needs. These needs are not merely wants or desires, but profound needs that form the basis of every choice and behaviour we make. As we come to understand those things that drive our behaviour, Tony believes we are better equipped to do the things that create feelings of success and happiness.

Tony and Cloé have defined six basic needs that we try to fulfill in our everyday lives. And, of these needs, (whether consciously or unconsciously), we will try to meet those that are deemed most important to us.

So what are these six basic needs, you ask? Let's take a look at them now. The first four needs relate to personality or achievement.

They are as Cloé explains :

"Certainty: The need for security, stability and reliability. This is our need to feel in control and know what's coming next. It's enables us to avoid pain and stress and, instead, create pleasure. It affects how much risk we are willing to take in life.

Variety/Uncertainty: The need for change, stimulation, and challenge. If you have too much certainty, you'll get bored. If you're not challenged enough, you'll stop learning. This need keeps life interesting.

Significance: The need to feel acknowledged, recognized, and valued for what you do. This is the need that keeps you wanting to achieve more out of life.

Love and Connection: The need to love, to feel loved, and to feel connected with others. They say "no man is an island", and it's very true. Our life is best lived in the company of others who will be there for us as much as we are there for them.

The final two needs relate to the spirit. They provide the structure for fulfilment and happiness. They are:

Growth: The need to grow, improve, and develop, both in character and spirit.

Contribution: The need to give, to help others and to make a difference."- Cloé Madanes

Discovering which needs are most important to us and how we try to meet those needs is an essential step towards achieving success and happiness. Or as Tony puts it on his website: "We don't value all six of the needs equally. Some have certainty as their top need. Some will have love and connection. Others may have significance. But whichever is number one is going to change the way you live your life."

In my world, I meet so many women who are seeking happiness through their homes. The biggest complaint is that the design of a home does not suit their lifestyle and they are embarrassed to entertain family and friends. When she speaks about how her home makes her feel, she uses words like anxious, agitated, dissatisfied, annoyed, bored, aggravated, frustrated, embarrassed, powerless, unhappy ... wow, that's a long list of negatives!

If these feelings are so powerful, then why are so many women reluctant to take action?

"Life is found in the dance between your deepest desire and your greatest fear" – Tony Robbins.

Here's how Tony sees it:

"We all have unlimited potential — but often our results don't reflect that. Why? Because our unconscious beliefs cripple our results. Our nature is to only invest energy into that which we believe will produce the outcome we seek. Therefore, when we believe something is not going to work out – even unconsciously – we sabotage our potential by taking halfhearted action. Little action equals lousy results. Lousy results equal uncertainty and disheartened beliefs. It is a vicious cycle that only ends when you decide to change what you're putting into it.

Potential. Action. Results. Beliefs. Certainty. Each word is fairly self-explanatory, but when we put them together to make the success cycle, we dive deeper into understanding the psychology of success. The more resolved beliefs we have about achieving something, the more potential we will tap. With greater potential comes greater action. Greater actions yield greater results. However, if we're not careful, the success cycle will also work in reverse. Beliefs have the power to create and the power to destroy.

But what is a belief, really? It's a feeling of certainty about what something means. The challenge is that most of our beliefs are unconsciously created based on our interpretations of painful and pleasurable experiences in the past. But the past does not dictate the present – unless you continue to live there. We can find experiences to back up almost any belief, but the key is to make sure that we are consciously aware of the beliefs we are creating. If your beliefs don't empower you, change them." – Tony Robbins.

Change Your Beliefs

In short, most of our beliefs are about ourselves, how the world works, and whether or not we deserve happiness. These are beliefs we acquired from our childhood experiences, and yet, like Karen, many of these beliefs or rules still run our lives as adults. Quite a few of them no longer serve us, and often cause us to unconsciously sabotage our success and our pursuit of happiness. Our minds keep us from taking certain actions, even though the actions may be reasonable and intelligent choices. Women, in particular, find themselves trying to fulfil needs that are not in line with their values and beliefs and, subsequently, they feel conflict and discontent.

Psychologists have a technical term for this. They call it "limited beliefs": beliefs that limit our ability to achieve our objective. No matter how much we wish to achieve something or how hard we try, they say, we do not really believe that we can achieve it so we're limiting our chances of success.

This extends to the idea of renovating and, in my experience, is particularly paralyzing to women. Just thinking about changing the look of one's home creates disempowering beliefs and a terror barrier, that keeps a woman awake at night as she battles with a desire to act, but also having an inability to break through voices in her head saying, "You're nuts. Don't bother!"

Trust me, you're not nuts! All you have to do is get past those limiting beliefs and you'll be just fine. In Tony's world, it's a three-step process that goes like this:

Change your state

Change your Story

Change your Strategy

In order to remove a limiting belief, it isn't enough to identify and acknowledge it. You may be aware of some of your limiting beliefs, but awareness isn't necessarily enough to make them happen. You may be aware that rejection isn't such a terrible thing, but your subconscious is still conditioned to avoid it. Awareness is an important part of the solution, but it isn't the whole solution.

Confession: I'm guilty of having limiting beliefs. When the thought first crossed my mind about writing this book, my subconscious took over and filled my mind with self-doubt and negativity. Why? Because I'm programmed that way from childhood. As I told Karen, I had low self-esteem as a kid. I believed that I should be seen and not heard. I had the limiting belief that I was not good enough or worthy enough to step out of my box and say what was on my mind. I was afraid of failure and the rejection and ridicule that came with that. And I suffered great pain because of it.

I really wanted to write. I was ready to throw off my mental shackles and live the life I was meant to live! But how?

Thankfully, a friend told me about Tony Robbins and how Tony's workshop changed his life. I Googled the guy and then ordered his book from the library. Interesting stuff! Soon I realized what "limiting beliefs" were and recognized instantly that I was suffering from them. As I learned from Tony, people will do more to avoid pain than to get pleasure. The fear of pain prevents us from moving forward. And we create rules when we're young that stay with us when we're older.

As daunting as it seemed, I made the effort to follow the steps required to make a shift to a more empowering belief. So I studied his six basic needs and followed his three-step process.

First, I had to change my state. I spent some time looking back on my life as a 10-year-old and all the hurt and pain and shyness that came with it. It wasn't easy to take myself back there, but I was determined to move forward. I questioned all the conclusions I had made when

I was a kid. I took hold of all the bad energy and worked desperately to change my state of submission from negativity to defiance. I took back my power by abolishing those subconscious thoughts and beliefs that prevented me from flourishing and, in doing so, I realized they had no place in my adult life. No place at all. Buh-bye! I would write that book that had long been inside me!

With that done, I was ready to change my story. I had to stop identifying with the belief that I could not write a book. I examined it, I challenged it, and finally, I laughed at it. And I created my new story. Hey, I had gained so much experience in the hows and whys of renovation over my 30 years in the construction and renovating business that my knowledge would be instrumental to anyone going through the process. Deep down, I knew I could make a difference. By changing my story, I knew I would make a difference.

Finally, I was able to change my strategy. I took responsibility, disconnected from my limiting beliefs, and took action. I identified the fears that were blocking me. Instead of my fears using me, I started to use the fears to motivate me. I created a plan with a schedule and goals. I turned my thoughts from "Should I write a book?" to "I must write a book!"

This was a big shift for me. And you know what? It opened a lot of new doors in all aspects of my life. I really do feel that the block is gone. My attitude shifted.

And here you are today, reading the fruits of my labour. I am worthy! I am knowledgeable! I am courageous! Hear me roar!

I am so grateful to Tony Robbins for helping me get to this point in my life. And that's why I like to pay it forward, as I did with Karen.

I got into this business to make a difference in my customers' lives. I want to help them take their lives to the next level by igniting their passion and happiness. I start off by engaging the customer with a meaningful conversation that helps them discover their needs and wants. To assist them, we discuss what their needs are and what limiting beliefs are preventing them from achieving their goals. By doing this, my customers liberate themselves from their subconscious negative beliefs and can achieve success and happiness.

Achieving happiness will change your life in many ways. However, you can't build everlasting changes until you create a balance and understand where your decisions stem from. Shifting your core foundation can help create healthier decisions from a place of wholeness.

Limited Beliefs Quiz

If you answer yes to ten or more of these questions then you have Limiting Beliefs:

1. I've had poor experiences with contractors in the past

2. I want to update my home but I don't know what the first step is

3. I feel like we should be making do with our home

4. A custom home is too much work and it's not something we truly need

5. I'm not sure I can afford a renovation

6. I don't want to live through a renovation and the mess and disorganization of it

7. I'm busy and don't have the time for a renovation

8. I don't know where to start a renovation

9. Renovations are too stressful

10. My day-to-day life will be uprooted during a renovation

11. I shouldn't be spending money on a home renovation

12. My friends and family will judge me for spending so much money on updating my home

13. I was raised to not take on any debt

14. I'm afraid if I update my home my friends will call me selfish

15. I was brought up with the "if it isn't broke, don't fix it" mentality

16. If I don't have the money upfront, it can't happen

17. Updating my home isn't a necessity

18. We have kids and should be saving for their future

19. A renovation won't increase the value of my home

20. I don't deserve a renovation

So, if you're wondering why you make the decisions you do, take Cloé Madanes's Six Human Needs Test. When you see your results, you'll be able to take the necessary steps to discover your true definition of happiness and, ultimately, ensure that your life fulfils your every need.

Take the Georgian Renovation

Human Needs Assessment Quiz

www.georgianreno.com/human-needs-assessment-quiz

Chapter 8

It's All About Lifestyle

"Til the one day when
the lady met this fellow
and they knew that it
was much more than a hunch
that this group must
somehow form a family..."

– Theme song from TV's The Brady Bunch

Three Keys to Renovation: Design, Design, Design

Another day, another home inspection! This time, I had the pleasure of meeting Sandra and Richard. Sandra had called me up earlier in the week and asked me to come over on Sunday afternoon. She runs a senior care business out of her home and he is the president of a Fortune 500 company. They're a blended Brady Bunch-type family with six children between them: two teenage girls, two teenage boys, and eight-year-old twin girls. They'd been living in Chicago until five years ago, when Richard was transferred to Toronto for work and they had just a few weeks to find a house that would be suitable for their brood.

It wasn't easy for them to find a house they both could agree on, she'd told me. They wanted a large lot with curb appeal (think stately exterior, spectacular entrance, two-car garage, manicured lawn, in-ground swimming pool). And with all those kids, they wanted as many bedrooms as possible plus a finished basement where the kids and their friends could hang out.

It was a tough order in such a short time. However, eager to start their new life, they chose to forgo renting until they found what they really wanted. Instead, Sandra and Richard purchased a large two-storey, four-bedroom subdivision home in a prestigious area of Mississauga.

Okay, so it only had four bedrooms, meaning some of the kids would have to share sleeping quarters. Still, it ticked off most of their needs. It was the right size, shaded by mature trees, had a pretty swimming pool, and was near good schools, designer malls, and was a short commute to Richard's new office. Sold!

Fast forward five years, and it simply wasn't working.

As I parked my car by the curb in front of the house, I noticed two hockey nets on the driveway and a basketball net suspended over the garage door. Clearly, their kids loved sports. The garage door was open so I couldn't help but notice that it was stuffed with furniture, boxes, and a ton of toys (no wonder the two cars were parked in the driveway). If they didn't hire me for a renovation, I thought, I'd try to entice them to tackle a garage makeover.

Sandra greeted me at the door with a big smile.

"Nice to finally meet you, Gene," she said as we shook hands. "Come in, but be careful where you step. I can't tell you how many times I've asked the kids to pick up after themselves. Richard's on a business call but he'll join us when he's done."

I followed her into the house, treading carefully around a jumble of sneakers, sandals, and boots of all colours and sizes. The living room, too, was littered with knapsacks, gym bags, balls, bats, and several team jerseys strewn on the couch and on the floor.

"Ah, I see I've come over at the same time as the football team!" I joked. Sandra giggled.

"Kids!" was all she said as I followed her into the kitchen. It, too, was a six-kid train wreck. The counter was cluttered with cereal boxes and plastic storage containers. The table was too big for the room and there clearly wasn't enough counter space. The kitchen table was covered with books, a couple of laptops and remnants of mid-after-noon snacks. In fact, the eating area was so tight that Sandra and the kids kept bumping into each other as they moved through it.

The family room had some challenges, too. There was an old brick wood-burning fireplace with smoke stains winding right up to the popcorn ceiling. One of the teenage boys was lying on a plush rug in front of a large 60-inch rear projection TV.

Then my eyes caught the ceiling. Sandra noticed.

"Ugly, isn't it?" she said, somewhat sheepishly. "The upstairs bathroom sprung a leak a few months back and now we've got these unsightly water stains on the ceiling. We had the leak fixed but there's some wood rot and mould that we should really take care of. But that's not why I called you over."

As we made our way upstairs, I could see space limitations were creating challenges here, as well. Typical of many kids' rooms, their floors were littered with clothes, towels, and shoes. Sandra hastily explained that she was always picking up after her kids. We stepped into the twins' room. The two little girls, Holly and Hannah, were sitting on the floor. One was brushing her Barbie doll's long hair and the other was threading colourful beads on a string. They both looked up and smiled.

"Are you the man who's going to fix our room?" asked Holly.

"I hope so!" I beamed.

I meant it. It was definitely too small for two growing kids and it didn't even have a closet. I mean, who builds a bedroom without a closet? The girls' clothes and belongings were crammed into a large, freestanding armoire that took up so much space that it partially blocked the doorway. "Some nights" said Sandra, gesturing towards the armoire, "it frightened Holly so much that she would climb into bed with Richard and I. They also complained for years that they had no privacy. They were desperate to have a functioning closet and a door that would close so they could lock out their older brothers who always teased them."

We moved on to the master bedroom. There was a freestanding clothes rack full of men's clothes and suits against one wall and a treadmill squeezed against the window of the other wall. The ensuite had one pedestal sink with an Ikea medicine cabinet right above it and an out-of-date Jacuzzi with a small one-piece corner shower.

When we returned to the kitchen table, our conversation was interrupted by one of the boys.

94

"Where's my math book, Mom? I can't find it anywhere," Before she could answer, we heard loud voices coming from the family room. Sandra sprung up from her seat.

"Adam, Melissa, enough already!" I heard her say. "Can't you see we have a guest? Why are you always fighting? One of you watch TV down here, and one of you go up and watch TV in my room." No doubt about it, this family was living in tight quarters and it was putting a strain on their relationships.

It felt like forever before Richard joined us in our shop talk. "I think it's pretty simple here," he said as we sat down at the kitchen table. "I think all we need to do to spruce up the place is fix the kitchen ceiling, repaint the master bedroom and the kids' rooms, wallpaper the powder room, and maybe switch out the living room and dining room carpeting for some hardwood flooring."

It became apparent that Richard had yet to see the true potential of their home and the opportunity to breathe new life into it. While I saw the need for a major makeover, he appeared happy to ignore the house's fundamental problems and was simply trying to fix the aesthetics. Like many homeowners, he had acclimatized to the problems of the house and the strain it put on the family's lifestyle.

"With Richard travelling a lot for work," said Sandra, "much of the family responsibilities fall on my shoulders. Despite the fact I run a business, I'm also a Carpool Mom Extraordinaire, shuttling the kids to school, hockey practice, basketball tournaments and gymnastics. I have a really hectic schedule trying to juggle all of this and still buy groceries, make dinner and oversee homework."

I was exhausted just listening to her. "How does the home make you feel?" I asked.

At that, Sandra sighed, let out a tired groan. "When we first moved from Chicago, the kids were younger and the house felt like it fit our lifestyle. We thought the house was almost perfect, but now it feels cluttered and dysfunctional. With so many teenagers, it's now bursting at the seams. We need to get rid of the chaos and bring some order and functionality to our lives."

I could see that it was frustrating for her to live in a home that was unsuitable for her family's lifestyle. There is nothing attractive about a cluttered home and a stressful life. Yet that was the environment that Sandra was living in day after day. I realized she was having a tough time explaining to me what she really wanted in terms of a renovation. She couldn't make up her mind, which I believed stemmed from her cluttered environment. How could a person even focus?

The best way to get clarity, I've found, is to declutter. It was high time Sandra let go of some of her stuff. I asked her to grab a pad of paper and start making a list of all the possessions that she could put into a garage sale. Then a second list of all the possessions that she could give away to charities. Then a third list of all the possessions she could throw away.

"You've got to let go of things," I advised. "It will not only clear your environment, but will clear your mind, too. Like a breath of fresh air. Start with the garage, then tackle the basement and eventually make your way from bedroom to bedroom. You don't need all that furniture you brought from Chicago that's taking up space in the garage. You don't need all those baby toys anymore that are still taking over your basement. Purge, I say, purge!"

I wanted to help her visualize a better, more functional and livable space. But we needed the whole family involved in this discussion. With her blessing, I called a family meeting. Richard and the kids were surprisingly intrigued.

"Designing a home is like embarking on an adventure," I told them. "My job is to help you take that adventure, but I can't make decisions about your ideal home without learning about what's on your wish list. So, my question is, if you could have the perfect home, what would it look like? What would you want to make it function better?"

Melissa was the first to jump in.

"The boys are always hogging the family room and it's got the only good TV," she groaned. "I'm too embarrassed to invite my friends over because their smelly hockey bags are all over the floor."

"I wish I had my own bedroom," piped up her sister, Caitlin. One of the boys nodded.

Indeed! Six children squeezed into three bedrooms didn't work at all. The floor plan was tight, but I knew I could solve this problem by creating a fifth bedroom upstairs and finishing off the basement with another bedroom and living area.

"I'd love a grand kitchen where we could host family and friends," said Richard. "One of those kitchens where the party happens and then spills out into the family room."

"Mom, you should get one of those walk-in closets," said Melissa.

"I'd love if we had a cool games room where we could fit in a pool table or maybe a theatre room for movie nights with my buddies and a bar area for parties," said Adam. "And maybe even a workout area and somewhere to jam with the guys or just listen to music."

I hear you, kid.

Particularly with a blended family, it's important that each set of kids has his or her own space where they can get away from the family, have some privacy and entertain friends on their own. Also, it could be a good place for family bonding. I immediately envisioned a large communal area in the basement and a great room on the main floor. Finally, Sandra spoke up.

"I wish I had a private office or library instead of working from a desk in our little bedroom," said Sandra.

"So, here's what I think," I said. "It's important that each of you have your own space to chill. And it's equally important to have somewhere to connect as a family. To do it right, we'd definitely have to enlarge the footprint of the house. The best solution is to add a bedroom over the garage. We'd create a stunning master bedroom to include a walk-in closet and beautiful ensuite with all the bells and whistles, giving you and Richard a perfect place to escape.

I continued. "On the main floor, we would expand the kitchen and open up some walls to give you an open concept where the entire family can be together. We'd reconfigure the main floor footprint to create a layout that makes sense for your busy family – by expanding the mudroom, relocating the powder room, bringing in an entirely new staircase while refreshing the entire home with new paint, flooring, trim and lighting."

They were hanging on to my every word.

"As for the basement," I went on, "we'd design the space to house everything your family needs, a grand recreational room complete with a sectional sofa, media centre, area for a games table finished off with a wet bar kitchenette, and a bedroom and bathroom retrofitted for your eldest teenage boy. And we'll even fit in a large fitness space with a glass wall!"

I could tell the kids were getting excited.

"And let's not forget all your stuff," I said finally, looking from one child to the next. "In order to keep all your clutter under control, I suggest building a large mud room with storage compartments, kind of like when you were back in kindergarten and you had your own cubby with your name on it!" They laughed. Sandra smiled, too.

I chatted with Richard and Sandra a little while longer. We talked skylights to bring in natural light and porcelain tiles for the kitchen floors and shower walls. Richard was enthusiastic about a great room just off the kitchen with a fireplace and a huge TV with surround sound. Sandra got excited about a main-floor study where she could do her work.

Lifestyle First, Design Second

When it comes to physical space, I've noticed one common theme: homeowners are rarely driven to renovate simply to improve the look of their home. Rather, they are usually motivated by a lifestyle change.

While all homeowners want a more attractive home at the end of the renovation project, their greater desire – whether they realize it or not – has to do with fixing things that are emotionally or psychologically anchored. This includes features such as:

Private space for finding solitude

Warm welcoming feel for entertaining and connecting with friends and family

A stylish or prestigious home that gives them a greater sense of pride

A soothing comfortable environment that lets the stresses of the day disappear after a hard day's work

More functional and less crowded living spaces that bring order to daily routine

An area in which the kids feel safe, can call their own and enjoy with friends

A home that reflects who they are as human beings and rises up to greet them when they walk in the door

Any successful renovation or custom home project relies heavily on identifying what lifestyle needs and desires are behind the homeowners' wishes for each particular space in the house. A successful project will satisfy or address several of these needs. That's why it's important for every homeowner contemplating a renovation to ask themselves the following question: "How have my family's lifestyle needs changed and how are they going to change or evolve in the future?" Then, and only then, should the design process move on to the physical attributes of the space.

Unfortunately, this first step in identifying and contemplating lifestyle goals is often ignored or skipped by many homeowners and their contractors. In these cases, people move directly into designing the space. This often results in renovation projects that don't achieve the aesthetic goals of the homeowner, that miss the opportunity to improve the lives of those living there, and that fail to adequately anticipate the changing needs of the family.

So how do you enhance your lifestyle by improving your home? How do you ensure your lifestyle needs are addressed with your renovation or construction project? Ask yourself the following questions:

Why are we renovating in the first place?

How do we spend our time?

What are our family's activities, sports, hobbies?

How do we like to live?

What are our entertaining habits and work habits?

What irritates me about my current home?
How can that be improved?

Are there any congested areas in my home? If so, where are they?

What do I want my home to say about me and my family?

I understand the importance of lifestyle and, therefore, treat it as a governing principle. Unfortunately, many contractors don't. They leave the task of understanding the process of design to the inexperienced homeowner, who is usually unaware of the intricacies and complexities of the design process.

Sandra's project is a case in point. In order to create a home that was perfect for her and her rambunctious family, I relied on the revolutionary design process created by Linda Petrin in her book Define Your Life, Design Your Home. It's a fascinating read! Linda teaches how to discover the unique attributes of your lifestyle and how to design your home for the way you live. This is a structured process that can actually change the way you live by changing the environment you live in. It allows us to design for a better lifestyle by connecting a home with that lifestyle.

In her book, Linda outlines three categories. Each category is comprised of seven lifestyle principles to guide personal expression in the design process:

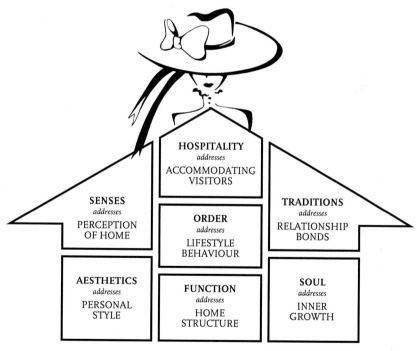

The 7 Lifestyle Principles

Category 1

Physical Principles – No matter what enticing extras a home may have (swimming pool, extra rooms, grand entrance), if a home does not fulfill your basic needs, you will have an adversarial relationship to the space. The physical principles ensure that the home fits your needs.

Order – Behaviour, activities, habits, and routines structure our lifestyle. A home with order enables these processes. Order is more than organizing and having the right containers: it is a relationship between our home and our behaviour.

Function – Every home must fulfill five human needs. First and foremost, a home must provide protection from intruders and the elements. We also need places to socialize and to pursue privacy, to eat and to sleep. Rooms must be the right size and provide the proper flow, offering a space plan that suits your lifestyle.

Category 2

Emotional Principles – When people think about design, they often think about how to make a space beautiful. The emotional principles are based on what makes us feel good.

Aesthetics – The ability to accumulate meaningful accessories and present them in an artistic manner is a source of great personal satisfaction.

Senses – Each sense registers a different experience. Together, all five create a synergistic encounter that is positive or negative. Rooms designed merely for what is seen fall flat and are quickly forgotten. Rooms designed for all our senses leave an impression.

Category 3

Spiritual Principles – Some activities produce personal growth and relationship bonds, reaching beyond just the physical or emotional. Consider the spiritual principles for a more meaningful life.

Soul – We need time, and our home needs places, to be alone and reflect, read, pray, meditate, sing, and just be. Soul places bring balance and clarity into our lives, thus improving the nature of who we are.

Traditions – Traditions satisfy our emotional need to belong and the home is an ideal place to establish and practice them.

Hospitality – Hospitality is sharing our homes and lives with others in whatever way we enjoy." – Linda Petrin

As Linda explains, the first six lifestyle principles focus on developing an environment and creating a lifestyle for everyone living in the home. The seventh principle (hospitality) defines who we have become and what we have to offer because of our lifestyle decisions and design efforts.

Construction of Sandra and Richard's addition took about six months. And, wow! What a difference! Their home was completely transformed with six bedrooms, six bathrooms, coffered ceilings, a formal dining room, a completed lower-level, a new office, and exquisite details throughout. The entrance foyer was spectacular, with a beautiful new staircase and a contemporary chandelier. The kitchen, with its stone backsplash and quartz countertops, was large, spacious, and perfect for entertaining, with plenty of space to mix and mingle. Sandra loved that her whole family could be together in one room, whether sitting at the island while she cooked or seated around the oversized sectional or just hanging out.

Sandra spared no expense on appliances by choosing the new top-of-the-line Sub-Zero fridge and freezer and a professional-style six-burner gas range to easily accommodate the endless number of meals she prepares, and a 72-inch, 178-bottle full-height wine cooler. They also went all out with an in-floor heated system covered by solid porcelain tiles imported from Italy which mimic the look and feel of reclaimed plank flooring.

On the second floor, the master bedroom had pocket-style sliding French doors, a dressing area, large walk-in closet, sitting area and gorgeous spa-like bathroom with a glass shower, freestanding vessel tub, floor-mounted faucet, heated floors, double sink vanity and oversized mirrors complete with inset wall sconces to add a touch of sparkle (quick, summon your Zen).

Over in the kids' "wing," everything was designed with the kids' personalities in mind by incorporating fun touches such as Swarovski crystal on the cabinet knobs and contrasting pink and white tiles in the girls' bathrooms and a mural of hockey great Sidney Crosby in one of the boys' bedrooms. As for the basement, I'd call it an entertainer's dream thanks to the bright and spacious games room, media room, and fabulous modern kitchenette/bar.

The renovation definitely captured the seven lifestyle principles:

Order

We organized Sandra's home around her living patterns and the needs of her active kids, with built-in storage millwork for in the laundry rooms, pantry, garage, bedrooms and great room.

Function

The new design allows the family to function well while meeting their needs for socialization and privacy. By removing the mould in the ceiling, we protected the family from infections. Their new great room was a perfect location for family to gather, watch television, do homework, cook meals, read books, and socialize. Holly and Hannah got their closet and their privacy.

Aesthetics

During my discussions with Sandra, I learned that she favours transitional style – a cross between traditional and modern, with soft lines and comfortable furnishings. By allowing Sandra to infuse her personal style into the design, she felt connected with their home and more comfortable living there.

Senses

Through colours, textures and trendy materials, we integrated the senses into the design to allow a deeper connection between the family and their surroundings. For instance, we used durable fabrics in the boys' rooms and "bling" colours in the girls' rooms.

Soul

The sitting area of the master bedroom allows Sandra to be alone so she can reflect, read or meditate. It's a place where she can recharge after a long busy day. We allowed for rituals by providing private spaces for all of the family members. Each of the children has his or her own private space to relax or entertain and Sandra has her own sitting area in her bedroom where she can escape and get away from it all.

Traditions

The large kitchen with the island provided a prime location where the family can bond while celebrating holidays, birthdays special occasions, or nothing at all.

Hospitality

The family was able to entertain their friends in the new open-concept kitchen that looks out to the great room.

As for the clutter ... what clutter? Though things still aren't perfect at Sandra's new place, everyone is working on becoming tidier thanks to the shoe racks in the laundry room and the storage compartments in the mud room and garage. The large pantry hides all of the non-stop snacks that the kids consume!

To me, this project satisfied the family's physical, emotional, and spiritual needs. Through it, I gained valuable insight into building for large blended families.

Questions to consider :

- How does your home reflect your current lifestyle?
- What does your home say about you and your family?
- What do you want your home to say about you?

Chapter 9

A New Man in Your Life

"You had me at 'Hello!'"

- Jerry Maguire

When I met Susan, a single 48-year-old high school teacher living in a two-bedroom townhouse in Hamilton, she'd just experienced a horrendous home renovation. When she discovered I worked in the home building and renovating business, she couldn't wait to share her horror story. I was more than happy to listen.

After living in her townhouse for several years, she'd decided she was tired of her drab 1990s style kitchen and main-floor bathroom. She wanted to gut the rooms and then remodel from scratch. Not knowing where to begin, she asked for referrals from relatives, friends and colleagues. The contractor who sounded most appealing was Gus, thanks to a glowing recommendation from a fellow teacher. She was impressed by him from their first telephone conversation and they set up a time to meet.

The moment she met Gus on her doorstep, looking dapper in his golf shirt and khakis, Susan was smitten. Tall, dark, and handsome in that Ryan Reynolds sort of way, he looked to be in his early 30s with a commanding presence and an engaging smile. He was so good looking, in fact, that she could feel the heat rise to her face as he introduced himself and shook her trembling hand. She confided to her friend later, that she couldn't believe how flustered he made her. It was like being on a first date!

Noticing her loss for words, Gus took control of the conversation right away. It was clear he was in charge. When they walked into the kitchen, he began asking questions.

"How much time do you spend in the kitchen?" he asked. "What do you like about it? What bothers you most? What's lacking? What's on your wish list? A classy lady like you must have a wish list."

She felt her cheeks heat up as he made eye contact with her. He was a good listener and seemed to respect what she was saying.

Susan told me that he had appeared to know a ton about countertops, shaker doors, handles and trendy sinks and light fixtures. She relayed that as he spoke, she imagined shopping alongside him at plumbing stores searching for that perfect sink and shining faucet. After all, wouldn't she need his professional advice to make the right choices? The more they chatted about her renovation, the more she felt that he valued her opinion and found her ideas interesting. He assured her that the renovation would go seamlessly. Then, with a few scratches of pen to paper, he produced an estimate for the job along with his "gorgeous, swoon-worthy smile" (her words, not mine).

Gus's confidence put her at ease, according to Susan. He was like a knight in shining armour come to rescue her from her kitchen distress. He seemed to understand exactly what she wanted to accomplish and understood her desire for a quick and painless job.

"I have another project I'm about to start," he had told her. "But I like your ideas and think it'll be an exciting project. If you decide within the week, I'll postpone the other one and take yours on first. I'll start working right away and you'll have your new kitchen and bathroom within six weeks!"

That was all Susan needed to jump right in. No checking his references or prior work. No checking to see if he was properly licensed. She agreed to his $50,000 price after a quick glance at the estimate, and signed on the dotted line. They agreed to meet the next day so she could give him a $15,000 deposit. He preferred cash but she insisted on giving a cheque.

It took Susan a few days to pack up her kitchen, clear out the bathroom and set herself up in her finished basement for the duration of the renovation. Gus showed up the next morning with a team and, as promised, the demolition began. She was thrilled!

Gus had warned Susan that kitchens have a long delivery time so the first thing that needed to be done was choose the kitchen details. That week Gus arranged for Susan to meet him at the local Home Depot store at 8 a.m. She arrived early, eager to select sinks, countertops,

tiles, colours, and cupboard knobs. Lo and behold, it was overwhelming! There were more choices than Susan had ever imagined; she
was grateful to have Gus by her side to expertly guide her through
the process. He seemed to know his stuff and she felt at ease with his
recommendations. Still, she wanted to check out some specialty shops
so they set up another "date."

They visited the flooring store and checked out exquisite porcelain
tiles. At the appliance store, Gus guided her through the features of
the modern stovetops, ovens, fridges and dishwashers on display.
Finally, he talked up the sinks and faucets in the plumbing showroom. He really cared about her porcelain, she could tell.
Of course she agreed with his recommendations. They just had that
kind of relationship. He would never steer her wrong.

For Susan, it was a blissful week and the relationship blossomed.
Susan and Gus shared coffee each morning and she enjoyed picking
up snacks and drinks for him and his workers during her lunch
break or after work. Gus became part of her daily routine and even on
weekends, she couldn't wait for his return visit.

Then one day, Gus didn't show up. Susan tried to quell that nervous
feeling in the pit of her stomach that had her wondering if he'd left
her for another renovation project. She was sure that he put her first.
The crew arrived, without him, to work on the drywall as she was
walking out the door. When she returned home, she found little had
been accomplished. Later that night, her neighbour called, furious
that a worker had blocked her driveway and then argued when she
confronted him. The next day, one of the workers cut an electrical
wire by accident, leaving Susan without power. Gus didn't answer her
calls or texts so she scrambled to find an electrician who could fix the
damage so as not to delay the reno timeline.

A few days later, Gus finally showed up. Susan fought the desire to
demand where he'd been. Was there another homeowner that he was
spending time with? She managed to calmly exchange pleasantries

over coffee until he turned their conversation to the renovation.

"The demolition has gone extremely well and we're on schedule," he enthused. "But there's a problem, Susan. The quote I received on the kitchen you want is double the price I'd quoted. And that sink you wanted so desperately? It's imported and turns out they gave us the wrong price. It's $1,800 more than I budgeted. So, I'll need another $10,000 in cash before I can order the kitchen and the sink. And once it's ordered, it then takes six weeks until it's ready to be delivered." Susan was stunned. Was this the same person she'd met at her doorstep who swept her off her welcome mat? Suddenly that smile seemed less genuine.

Sensing her disappointment, Gus was sympathetic but firm. "Without the extra money, I can't order the kitchen and we can't proceed with the work. I'll need that up front, in cash."

While she was still fuming over his news, Gus delivered the clincher. His mother, who lived overseas, was ill and wanted him by her side. He'd booked a flight for the next evening and would be gone for at least two weeks. But he'd have his workers on the case and one of his men would supervise so she shouldn't worry. Naturally, there would be a slight delay with the project, he told her, though he assured her not to worry. She'd be thrilled with the final results.

Susan was aghast. Not only was her budget ballooning, but he was leaving it in the hands of those messy men? In that instant, Susan finally saw past his good looks. She'd paid so much money upfront and now felt like a hostage. She'd heard about renovations gone bad. Was hers going to be one of them? She hoped not. Ending the contract was out of the question now. There was too much at stake.

She agreed to his new terms and gave him the money. The workers didn't show up for three days and, once they did, they progressed slowly. The so-called "boss" wasn't responsive to her questions about their process and next steps. With Gus gone, Susan took on the role of overseeing the job and was the one to push them along, call them out on their shabby workmanship and organize timelines. When she retreated at night to her cold basement, she couldn't rest easy because she was second-guessing their work and had nobody to turn to for guidance.

Once back in the country, Gus didn't show up for over a week, nor did he answer any of her texts or phone calls. He had been overly attentive before she paid him his first deposit. But now, he had disappeared. Was this the same man who called her three times a day when they first met?

When he finally arrived on her doorstep three weeks after he'd bid her adieu, the project was weeks behind schedule and the house looked like a war zone. He had more bad news: there were extra costs that he hadn't expected and she'd have to pay up. Again.

Susan got angry. And boy, did Gus feel it. She knew her project was not the only one but she still thought she was special. His broken promises disappointed her. She had trusted him and he had betrayed her. Her adoration turned to seething rage. Her faith in Gus was shattered. She detested him.

And she was mad at herself, too. Why hadn't she done her due diligence on him before handing him over her hard-earned savings? How dumb could she have been for signing the estimate? She should have known better!

Okay, so she had no idea about the ins and outs of a renovation ... but that's why you hire an expert, right? She never thought that a nightmare job would happen to her. She'd been charmed by Gus's good looks, his calm bedside manner, and the halo she'd perceived hovering over his head. Now, after experiencing so much frustration, anger and panic, she wanted to wrap that halo around his neck!

Finding the Perfect Match

The single most important person on your team is the contractor. Hiring the right person for the job is the single most important thing you can do to set up your project for success. While more and more women are entering the business of home renovation my comments can also apply to women but they are more directed towards the male contractors who are more prevalent in the renovation business in Toronto.

I empathized with Susan when she told me her story, but truth be told, her story is all too typical of a renovation gone bad. Alas, many people have little or no understanding of how the renovation process works or what to look for in a contractor.

You and your contractor spend a lot of time together. It's not a casual relationship. You may see the contractor first thing in the morning, after a hard day at the office, or after a long day with the kids. With that in mind, finding someone with whom you feel comfortable working is important.

It is important to draw a line in the relationship. Striking a balance between a friendly yet business-like rapport with a contractor often becomes a challenge as you get to know each other better and see each other frequently. If you can maintain a balance, you will have a much easier time dealing with problems as they arise.

Before Signing "I Do"

Home-improvement fraud is a common complaint of the Better Business Bureau, with scores of shady contractors across the country making headlines for defrauding homeowners.

Fortunately, for all the incompetent or unscrupulous contractors out there, there are just as many highly professional, dependable, ethical contractors who do a good job for you. The right person for the job is definitely out there!

Most contractors have honest intentions, but that doesn't mean that they are good or competent. Unfortunately, incompetent contractors are extremely common. A good contractor must be a solid business person who is organized and has technical, administrative, and interpersonal skills. An ability to keep track of every detail associated with the job is paramount to maintaining high quality standards while staying on schedule and on budget.

But it's not just about the paperwork. Your contractor must be a good manager of people to coordinate and manage the efforts of the sub-trades and work well with the rest of the team. Your project will be in trouble if your contractor misses details, fails to pay subcontractors, or suppliers on time and treats workers poorly.

Your whole project could suffer when the following happens:

Contractor underestimates the job: If he makes an educated guess on the cost of the project, rather than pricing it properly, he will end up cutting corners or charging more later on.

Contractor can't get his act together: If he is disorganized and cannot coordinate schedules, the project will get delayed.

Contractor two-times you: If he has multiple jobs going at the same time and doesn't have the experience or manpower to manage them properly, expect problems. He will often pull subcontractors off of your job to deal with problems on his other jobs.

Contractor isn't experienced enough: He may think he can handle your large job because he has some experience on smaller jobs but it will soon become obvious that he's in over his head on a big project.

Contractor doesn't work well with others: If he isn't capable of work-ing effectively with his team or managing subcontractors day-to-day, the result will be miscommunication, low morale and, ultimately, shoddy workmanship and delays.

Contractor wheels and deals: If he can't manage his finances well, he will be behind in paying his bills and that, in turn, will cause serious problems. For example, he might take your deposit in order to get your job going while also using it to pay for materials on another job, leaving him scrambling on both projects.

Finding "The One" Takes Time

For major renovations, additions, and custom homes, I recommend that you rely on larger contracting businesses with the capacity to take on complex projects. They employ, or are affiliated with, professionals such as structural engineers, architects, and designers. Small projects without any structural changes can be managed by a small contractor who performs the work himself, as long as he has the necessary skills and qualifications.

The advantage of hiring a larger company is they will have multiple crews, each dedicated to their own specific project. These crews have a dedicated supervisor who usually gets things done quickly and with good quality.

When looking for a contractor, it's critical to do thorough research and get references. Otherwise you may end up hiring a take-the-money-and-run type of guy who will rip you off or do poor quality work.

When you're dating, some matchmakers are more reliable than others. Similarly, when seeking a referral from someone you know, be cautious. Consider the referrer's relationship with the contractor. Is the referral really based upon the confidence or familiarity with the contractor's work?

Who you can rely on for good referrals?

Realtors are a good source of referrals because they have experience with contractors who have done good jobs for the clients.

Subcontractors know who the good contractors are: the ones who produce quality work and pay them on time.

Architects and designers often work with contractors on a regular basis so they know who does a good job and who does not.

Internet sites are good starting point for your search. Be wary of contractors who do not have a web page.

The First Date

Interviewing prospective contractors can be time-consuming and exhausting. It may be tempting to fall for the first one you meet, especially if he's overly charming! However, it's important to meet other people so you have a basis for comparison before you settle on The One. The investment of time and energy will be worth it down the road. As an added bonus, you may get some good design ideas from the contractors you don't end up hiring.

In that first meeting, it's important that you take charge and demand the contractor's respect. Since you've already done your homework, think of this meeting as an audition by asking lots of questions to ensure your research and his answers match.

Here are some important questions to ask at this meeting:

Are you licensed? Show me your license.

What industry associations do you belong to?

What type of projects have you handled in the past?

How many projects can you handle at the same time? If I hire you, how many projects will you have on the go at the same time?

Do you use crew leaders and superintendents?

Do you have a professional project manager in the office?

How long have you been in business?

Do you work with your own crew or do you use subcontractors? Is everyone licensed?

Do you have an office and, if so, do you have an office manager?

How much time will you spend at my home supervising the project?

How often do you clean up?

Do you have a safety program in place? If so, what does it entail? If not, why not?

Who will be in charge of getting the permits and inspections?

Will you provide a written contract?

What is your HST business number?

Do you have liability insurance?

Can you provide Workers Compensation clearance?

Can you provide several names and numbers of client references?

Once you've conducted several thorough interviews, take your time to consider who is the best fit. Some contractors will pressure you to make a commitment at the first meeting. They will give you an on-the-spot price and ask you to sign their estimate.

Even if you love what you've heard, don't sign anything! The first date is no time to make a commitment. An estimate is not the same thing as a detailed quote. An estimate given during the first meeting is, at best, very rough. Signing it might be interpreted as a contract between you and the contractor: it is not.

Signer Beware!

Just because your contractor has done similar work in the past doesn't mean the two of you will click. Look for warning signs that could spell trouble for you down the road. Here are some of the most prevalent red flags:

- He's late for the first meeting

- He isn't licensed

- He doesn't have insurance

- He seems uncomfortable about giving you names of previous clients or refuses to do it at all

- He puts pressure on you to hire him right away

- He's intimidating, condescending, impatient, disrespectful, and makes you feel uneasy in any way

You've heard the expression "you get what you pay for." This saying is never more relevant than when you're hiring a contractor for a home improvement or remodeling project. Going by price alone increases the risk of project failure and can lead to higher costs down the road.

The trade association, RenoMark (www.renomark.ca), is an excellent place to start. All of its members have agreed to a code of ethics which includes extended warranty and written contracts.

The Prenuptial Agreement

Much like a marriage contract, a contractor-homeowner relationship requires a prenuptial agreement of sorts. In this case, it's called a written contract.

Don't make the mistake of sealing a deal on a handshake. Without a written contract, you will be vulnerable to all sorts of things that can go wrong with a renovation project including ballooning budgets, worker injury claims or shoddy workmanship.

Before you tie the knot with your contractor, take a close look at the "prenup" contract to ensure it contains the following:

Valid company name: It must be in the name of a legal entity (such as a corporation, partnership or a personal name) for it to be binding.

Contact information: It must list the name, address, phone number, email address and phone number of the construction superintendent.

Contractor's municipal license number.

HST number: Contracts that do not adhere to HST payments are illegal and customers will be liable for the payments and fines.

Workers Compensation number: Without this coverage, the homeowner will be responsible for the costs of any injured workers' insurance claims.

Liability insurance binder: This provides protection against property damage. The contractor must provide proof of coverage prior to starting the work. Homeowners need to notify their insurance company of the pending renovation.

Description of the project and scope of the work: The contract should spell out what work will be done. All plans and specifications must be attached.

Material selections list: The contract must contain a detailed list of all materials, brand names, colours, model numbers, etc. that will be used to complete the project. Without this, the homeowner will be leaving it up to the contractor to choose and, therefore, relinquishing control over quality.

Allowances: If certain items have not been selected prior to entering into the contract, a contractor may allow an amount allocated for items be selected by the homeowner.

Who is responsible for permits: The property owner is responsible for complying with all permit requirements. The contract should specify that the contractor apply for and obtain all required permits and inspections. If the project does not comply with the building, electrical, plumbing, or gas codes, the building department can force the homeowner to correct any deficiencies in the work or demolish it.

Contract Price: The contract price has to be clearly stated.

Payment terms: Installment payments need to be specified and geared to the progress of the work.

Change order procedure: It doesn't matter how much planning goes into the project because a change in plans is inevitable. Therefore, the contract must provide for a procedure to make changes to the contract's terms.

Holdback release procedure: Before the final payment is released to the contractor, a homeowner will want to ensure that the contractor has completed the work, provided all warranties, and cleaned up the home properly so that it's ready for occupancy.

Hiring a contractor for a major renovation is a serious commitment. Rushing into a decision can spell doom for your home, your well-being, and of course, your wallet. Take your time, be thorough, and select a contractor that you firmly believe will lead your renovation professionally from start to finish.

Renovation Score Card

Use the below quiz to evaluate each professional you talk to, rating them from 1 to 10 and tallying the results for a final rating.

Company Name ....

Is communication comfortable and open?

1   2   3   4   5   6   7   8   9   10

Is the company transparent about their processes? Can they explain in detail how the process will work from start to finish?

1   2   3   4   5   6   7   8   9   10

How are the ratings and reviews from past customers?

1   2   3   4   5   6   7   8   9   10

Do they offer a warranty? If so, what are the terms?

1   2   3   4   5   6   7   8   9   10

Do they have a website? How professional does their website?

1   2   3   4   5   6   7   8   9   10

Do they provide a written contract? How extensive is it?

Do they have experience in similar projects?

1   2   3   4   5   6   7   8   9   10

Chapter 10

The Architect as Hero: Myth or Reality?

"Looking for something we can rely on. There's got to be something better out there."

– Tina Turner, We Don't Need Another Hero

Cheryl and her husband, Stuart, bought their spacious two-storey, ravine-lot home in Forest Hill when their two kids were small. But 15 years later, they craved more space and an update without having to move. Since they weren't sure where to begin, Cheryl called around to a few of her friends who had already renovated and asked them for advice on how to get the process going.

"First up is the architect," her friends told her. "Try James. He's pretty good. He's a bit pricey but he knows his stuff."

Cheryl had seen James's signs on properties around the neighbourhood and had been impressed by his website, so she placed the call. Clearly a busy professional, it took James a few days to reply. She didn't mind because she'd heard such terrific things about him. As soon as she told him what street she lived on, she could sense his delight.

"Oh, that's one of my favourite streets in the city," exclaimed James. "I've done quite a few projects there over the past few years. Can't wait to hear what your plans are!"

Once Cheryl explained her wish list, James seemed to know exactly what she was talking about. His enthusiasm put her at ease. No doubt he was experienced, given his reputation, so she didn't ask him too many questions. They agreed to meet at the house three weeks later.

James was as personable in person and he had a commanding presence that felt reassuring to Cheryl. After touring him around the house, Cheryl and Stuart discussed the wish list in more detail over peppermint tea.

"Here's what I'm thinking," he said. "You've got a fabulous space here but you're right, it really deserves a fresh new look. To get the most out of it, let's remove the roof and replace it with a higher pitched, more elegant one. We'll extend the footprint out the back and front to add more space. And let's really make the entryway pop with a two-storey grand foyer with a skylight. It will be spectacular!"

"Yes, that would be gorgeous, don't you think, Stuart?" she asked, looking dreamily at her husband. "All that extra space would make such a difference now that the kids are older."

"It sounds fantastic," Stuart replied. "But listen, James, we're prepared to spend $500,000 on the addition and not a penny more."

"No problem!" James said. "That sounds like a perfect budget for this type of project. That's definitely doable. If we're on the same page, I can start on the drawings on Monday and have them to you in a couple of weeks. Then, once you sign off on them, we'll submit them to the city for approval and your contractor can get started. My cost for initial drawings is $40,000. All I'll need for you now to get going is your signature on the contract and a retainer of $10,000 and we'll be good to go."

Three weeks later they met again, this time in James's office. After approving the design, James requested the balance of the payment so he could submit the drawings for a building permit. They paid him and then went out for a drink to celebrate their soon-to-be renovated home.

Shortly thereafter, Stuart received a phone call from Tony, the office manager of the architect's office.

"I'm afraid I have some bad news," Tony said. "The house backs on to a ravine, right? Well, we've been notified by the building department that the rear addition was designed too close to the top of bank of the ravine. Not only that, but the street has a special zoning bylaw for height restrictions and the proposed design contravenes the height restriction by three feet." Stuart was perplexed.

"What are you telling me?" he asked. "You mean the drawings are no good?"

"They'll have to be amended. Call James and see what he can do."

"You bet I will!" Stuart said, his voice rising. He put down the phone and immediately called James.

"Oh, that's too bad," said James when he heard the situation. "The height restriction bylaw is very difficult to get around. We could apply to the Committee of Adjustment for a minor variance to get around this restriction. As for the rear addition, we could apply for relief from the setback, too."

"Isn't that something you'd have looked into before submitting the drawings?" Stuart asked, trying to keep calm. "Why didn't you check it out earlier?"

"Well, we've done work in your neighbourhood before and never faced this problem before," muttered James. "I'll have to charge you to apply for the variances."

"Seriously?" Stuart retorted. "More money?"

"Yes," James replied calmly. "I'm afraid it's just par for the course when you do business with the city."

Stuart was agitated. But what could they do? It had to be done. Their hands were tied.

"Okay then, James, charge my Visa. You have the number. Get it done as soon as possible. But for heaven's sake, make sure you have all the information you need before you submit the new drawings."

"Will do!"

It took four months to get an appointment with the Committee of Adjustment. Several of the neighbours showed up and made it clear that they disapproved of the roof height variance. By the end of the hearing, the Committee sided with the neighbours but did allow a partial variance on the setback. Then it was back in James's hands.

"Okay," he told Cheryl and Stuart over a post-hearing coffee at a nearby coffee shop. "We can chop off the top three feet of the roof and create a flat roof, which will still give us the space we need to maintain the addition. All we have to do is reconfigure the dimensions and rework the interior to achieve a similar result."

"What's that going to cost?" Stuart snarled.

"$40,000," said James. Stuart and Cheryl looked at each other, aghast.

"But that will mean we'll have paid you double what you asked for when we signed the original contract," exclaimed Stuart. "That's insane! Why should we have to pay for something that you should have known in the first place?"

"Like I told you, Stuart, it's the cost of doing business with the city. Now that we have some concrete answers, I'm happy to rework the plans. I'm so sorry for the inconvenience but just like you don't work for free, neither do I."

Cheryl let out a sigh, her eyes welling with tears. Stuart could tell by the look on her face how disappointed she was. He was more angry than disappointed. The design costs had ballooned – unnecessarily, in his opinion – and six months had gone by. But having spent all this money and time already, it wouldn't make sense to start from scratch with someone else. Again, their hands were tied.

"Okay, James," said Stuart. "But just know that we're not happy. Not one bit."

Three months later, the building permit was finally approved and issued. James invited four contractors to submit bids for the project. Unfortunately, only two picked up the drawings for tender and only one, a contractor named Harry, quoted for the job. His quote: $900,000 – almost double what Stuart and Cheryl had been willing to spend.

"Don't worry," James assured them. "I know Harry personally and he's terrific. I'd really recommend sitting down with him even though he's more expensive than you'd expected."

Once again, it was peppermint tea around the kitchen table. According to Harry, they could reduce costs by $100,000 by nixing the grand foyer and the front two-storey addition. If they agreed, they'd have to go back to the drawing board (literally!) and pay James to redesign the plans yet again.

"As owners, you're responsible for accuracy, errors and omissions of all the information provided to the contractor, which I will rely on in preparing my proposal," he said, pulling a standard construction contract from his briefcase and placing it on the table. "That means accuracy of the drawings and information provided by the architect." James noticed that the architect was not a party to the contract. So, the cost of any mistake was on his shoulders.

A year after James's first visit, work on the house finally commenced. By then, Stuart and Cheryl and the kids had moved into a rented apartment and were making the best of a tight situation. But as things got going, there seemed to be an ongoing parade of change orders from the contractor as he uncovered what he felt were a slew of mistakes and errors with the drawings.

For instance, none of the finishes were selected in the project drawings. James claimed that would have been an interior designer's responsibility, which his contract did not include. In the absence of a finishing schedule, Harry had provided allowances for each of the finishes, which were all lowballed for quality and selection. Cheryl was forced to spend days at kitchen showrooms, tile and plumbing showrooms and appliance showrooms. She dragged a reluctant Stuart to all of the showrooms on weekends, cutting into what he felt should be time spent relaxing or doing family activities. Suffice it to say that his wife had expensive taste so they were going over budget yet again.

As for Harry and James, they kept on blaming each other. It was a constant battle between them with never-ending finger pointing.

Neither one of them wanted to accept responsibility.

Stuart felt that James should have provided the interior design services and negotiated all of the change orders. James disagreed, saying that he was not contracted with them to provided interior design services or to administer the construction. If he had, his fee would have been $50,000 for interior design services and 10% of the construction cost for construction administration.

"Clients don't want to pay for those services so I don't include them in my fee proposals," he said.

At that, Stuart exploded. "Look here!" he said, thanking his lucky stars that they were on the phone or he'd have socked James in the face. "When we first met, you said we could have our dream home for $500,000. You somehow forgot to mention that your fees don't include interior design services or construction administration services. You should have known about all the zoning laws and designed accordingly from the get-go. I spent days managing the extras on the construction and negotiating with both you and the contractor. It's taken a toll on my business and my wife and I are constantly stressed out. We've had to extend the lease on our rented apartment four times and we still have no idea when our so-called 'dream home' will be ready. It's been hard on me, on Cheryl and the kids. If you'd have done your job properly in the first place, we wouldn't be in this mess! I'm seriously thinking of reporting you to the Better Business Bureau. If there's one thing I've learned, it's that I now hate architects!"

When I first heard the story, Stuart didn't tell me what James said to that, and I didn't ask. I was worried Stuart's head would explode if we kept talking about it.

I'd like to say that this case is unique, but it is all too common. Homeowners often hire an architect because they believe it's the responsible plan of action when considering a major renovation. Almost inevitably, they pay the architect a pile of money to develop plans with no promise of actually building it. Then, it is assumed they'll find a qualified contractor willing to speculate their time to undercut each other in a bidding war and offer a cheap enough price that the homeowner may actually afford to build the architect's vision.

It sounds counterintuitive but before you look for an architect to design your new project you should choose a builder first.

Why?

Well, did you know that 80% of architectural plans never come to fruition?

You see, an architect focuses on what a home will look like, the design. The problem is, they rarely factor in the cost, so often, you end up with a design that will become too expensive to build. Architects are trained to be visionaries. They live to create the perfect house. That's what you pay them for, but they are not focused on the practicalities of building. The reality is that they get paid for the design they create, whether you use it or not.

The better alternative is using a design build process. A professional design-build firm is comprised of in-house designers, each of whom have a Building Code Identification Number (BCIN), professional engineering services, and an interior designer, all of whom specialize in residential projects. By combining the service and expertise of these experts into one unified service, the architect/designer and the contractor are able to work together as one cohesive team in a synergistic way. This typically results in a more effective process from beginning to end, with fewer changes during construction. It also results in a happier and more satisfied client.

I have nothing against architects. Really! I have worked with them for years and I've even made friends with a few of them. But based on my experience, they're just not good at pricing things out. They lack estimating skills and are not current with product costs. They dictate design and force their favourite style or award-winning vision on their clients without giving any thought to costs. As for contractors, they are so busy that few have the time or the desire to gamble or speculate on a bidding war that they might lose.

In Ontario, the term "architect" can only be used by someone who is accredited by the Ontario Association of Architects (OAA). Architects are broadly trained in the design of all types of buildings - including skyscrapers, institutional, and multi-residential buildings - but they are not always experts in home design and few specialize in the niche area of single-family home additions and renovations. Architectural firms tend to focus on larger projects and are less likely to have extensive experience with the unique challenges related to renovating and expanding old homes.

Myth vs. Reality

Let's look at some of the myths surrounding working with an architect:

Myth: Architects have control over the project's budget

Reality: Architects have no control over the budget. The OAA has strict policies limiting how its members can offer services. It also precludes them from selling combined design and construction services to the public in order to avoid conflict of interest and to maintain a level of independence as professional consultants serving the best interests of their clients. Because of these stipulations, hiring an architect becomes expensive, time-consuming, and complicated. It's not the responsibility of the architect to deliver a design that meets the homeowner's proposed budget.

Myth: Only architects can design houses and make applications to municipalities for home renovation building permits

Reality: Anyone accredited as a house designer by the province of Ontario and has a Building Code Identification Number (BCIN) can also make building permit applications. BCIN-qualified designers are specialists in residential design and architectural technology. They are trained to deliver cost-effective, efficient one-stop-shop planning, design, and execution of an addition or renovation. If you like the idea of dealing with a single responsible party guiding you from start to finish and providing direct accountability for your satisfaction throughout the whole process, then an architect might not be right for you.

Myth: An architect will manage the construction process from start to finish

Reality: Construction administration is a very expensive additional service not normally included in an architect's fees. The OOA's Standard Short Form of Contract for Architect's Services (Form #OAA 800-2011) clearly states the list of an architect's scope of services. The client must select each service that is required from the architect: design, construction documents, permits and approvals, negotiating, bidding phase, construction contract administration, or any combination thereof. Most homeowners are in a hurry and only want to pay the architect enough to acquire the building permit. They want to save money so they engage the architects for partial service contracts, but that spells trouble. It's more important to engage one for a full-service contract that includes: preparation of the schematic designs, design development, detailed construction documents and specifications, and overseeing the tendering and negotiation stage as well as the construction administration stage. Typical fix fees for full-service architectural contract range from 10 to 20% of the construction costs. Not paying these fees could result in obtaining incomplete drawings.

Myth: An architect's design will reflect what the homeowner can afford

Reality: Many homeowners have blind faith that the architect can magically make things cheaper. They also trust that the architect will provide drawings that are complete and accurate. But, in actuality, there is usually so much information missing from the drawings that it makes the notion of a Lump Sum Price Contract laughable. Once a contract is signed with the contractor, they usually pour over the drawings with their team to find all the mistakes, errors, and omissions and then have to charge the homeowner for the change orders. And once the contract is awarded, the homeowner is stuck having to accept the contractor's inflated charges without the benefit of comparison or time. Until the change order is approved, the project will sit idle and the homeowner owner will be responsible for any extended duration charges issued by the contractor.

The Wrong Way to Do It

Here's a typical step-by-step scenario of how a project that begins with hiring an architect usually goes down. I've seen it happen often.

A client hires an architect to design and specify his dream project according to his needs and desires and then pays for the work.

The architect completes the design.

The client doesn't pay attention to the details of the plan because they believed they hired an architect who covers every aspect of the plan.

The client puts the work out to tender to several rival general contractors to actually turn the design into reality by constructing a project according to the drawings: that is, if the project cost did not exceed the anticipated budget.

The contractors find problems with the design, and so are overly optimistic in pricing.

The client decides to not pay the extra architectural fees to spec out and fix every detail.

The contractor lowballs the tender by excluding important items of the work or substituting parts of the work with cheaper sub-standard products. He eithers guesstimates the cost of the project or rejects the job outright.

The client chooses the lowest price from the most optimistic (read: most unrealistic) contractor.

Work begins.

During construction, the client is charged extra for all the unexpected work necessary due to the architect's initial design.

The client feels there is no choice but to agree to the extra charges.

Due to the higher project costs, the client must give up part of their proposed dream home in order to build something they can afford.

Disappointment sets in.

The building process continues as a series of change orders and ongoing negotiations filled with conflict. The adversarial environment finds each party defending their positions to build the project while protecting their own financial interests.

By the time the project is complete – over budget and well beyond the promised timeframe – the client is so stressed that he can't immediately enjoy the home.

This process is broken. It requires more of the homeowner's time and effort to manage the relationship between the architect and the contractor. Conflict is virtually assured. Since there is no single party responsible for the client's satisfaction from start to finish, the client's expectations are unlikely to be met. In fact, they might end up in court.

Design-Build: The Knight in Shining Armour

Have no fear, friends! There is a better way to a more collaborative approach that is based on trust rather than fear.

Two words: Design-Build.

Every great design begins with a well-thought-out plan that should begin with the client's vision.

With a design build team the process is evolutionary. Each design begins with a concept sketch that lacks detail but helps organize the client's wish list. In some cases, it takes more than one drawing to nail down the concept. Design then evolves into larger-scale architectural drawings that are more detailed and clearly define all of the spaces, dimensions and selections. Finally, the process proceeds to construction drawings in which special details are developed and incorporated into the design. As the design evolves, it will increasingly fit the client's needs.

Warning: don't get put off by the first set of drawings! They will likely be only 75% on target. As the project moves into the actual construction drawings, the design is refined to the point of being about 90% on target. The last 10% of the evolution takes place with the final refinements during construction. Be sure to set aside contingency funds to cover changes that are made during construction.

Good design process must include estimating the actual construction cost at every phase of the evolution. In the concept stage, the estimate is a fuzzy or preliminary number in need of refinement as the drawings are defined. At this stage, it is best to consider an elemental budget to see the direction of where the budget is going. As the design evolves into future phases, the estimate, like the design, will get tighter and more accurate. Each version of the design is an opportunity to get closer to the proposed budget. The design-build team is the best possible resource in this process for developing estimates and ideas and presenting the options and merits of these options in all aspects of the design evolution.

There are many external factors that will affect the outcome of your design process and, ultimately, your budget. This includes:

easements, architectural controls, site plans, setbacks, zoning issues, soil constraints. Furthermore, your ability to acquire proper financing is a key factor as well. It's a good idea to speak with your banker or mortgage broker before beginning the process so you to get a firm handle on your funding ability and what you can realistically afford.

Design-build has become extremely popular because it eliminates many of the common problems, frustrations, setbacks, and delays associated with the traditional approach.

When hiring a design-build firm, the contractor provides a single point of accountability who guarantees the design, the price and warranty, and is directly accountable to the client for the entire process. The client states the project's budget upfront, enabling the budget to drive the design process. The design is completed with every detail and real pricing for all the materials, labour, supervision, profit, and overhead. In other words, the project is completely priced before it is started. If costs are beginning to exceed the anticipated budget, adjustments in scope or budget can be made. The team is committed to using its creativity to ensure that the client gets the best product for the lowest price.

Not all architects are as villainous as James. Architects can add value to the right project with the right scope of work and with the right customer. The alternative to an architect is the Design-Build team who are in my book the "Reno Heroes" of the renovation world. The Reality is that a Design-Build team can avoid renovation disasters with their stress- free process that makes the dreams of homeowners a reality.

Gene's Top 10 Benefits to a Design-Build Process

10. Everyone's on the same team

9. Sole-source accountability without finger-pointing

8. Construction is faster

7. Design is more creative and innovative

6. Cost control of budgeting and value engineering

5. Customer involvement with more choices

4. Guaranteed fixed price

3. Transparent communications

2. Better quality

1. Client's risk is reduced

Questions to consider:

Is your project large enough to require
the use of a professional architect?

Do you think it's worth it to pay an
architect to supervise and manage the project?

You understand the value of a design build project?

Chapter 11

Renovate and Get Rich

"Don't tell me I can't do it. Don't tell me it can't be done!"

– Leonard DiCaprio as Howard Hughes, The Aviator

When 40-somethings Dana and Kevin decided to move in together after four years of dating, they faced a major hurdle finding a home. In the overheated housing market in Toronto, entering the fray is not for the faint of heart. With house prices galloping ahead, their dream of buying a home seemed less and less attainable. The couple simply needed a place large enough to accommodate their blended family, which included five children ranging in age from 9 to 17.

Blended families that include children of a previous marriage of one spouse or both now make up almost 13% of Canada's 37 million families with children, according to figures from the 2011 Census. This says a lot about the changing family landscape in this country. What was once a rarity has become the new normal. With it comes the challenge of finding adequate living arrangements.

Dana had noticed one of my company signs on a house down the street and had kept an eye on the project. She had received a letter in her mailbox from our company informing the neighbourhood about the starting of a renovation and apologizing in advance for any inconvenience or dust. She appreciated our good neighbour policy and noticed how clean we kept the construction site.

"I made a point to go over and speak to the couple who owned the home and ask them about you," said Dana, a Harvard educated psychology professor at York University. "They had nice things to say including that you were honest with your pricing. They are glad you convinced them to set a realistic investment range because they ended up getting everything on their list."

The couple invited me into the home and explained that their motivation for the renovation was to ensure the children had their own bedrooms and common areas.

"Suddenly, we were doubling our family size," said Dana, "How do you make that work in a busy city like Toronto with two busy parents working insane hours? To buy a five-bedroom home in a midtown address even partially renovated, you are looking at two to three million dollars. That's insane! The ones we liked, in our price range, we're not even close to being big enough. And anything large enough, needed a lot of work, which was out of our price range."

At the time they had decided to move in with Kevin, Dana was living with her two boys in the three-bedroom side split in Etobicoke that she and her ex-husband purchased 15 years ago. Meanwhile, Kevin, now her husband and a gynecologist with a busy uptown practice, was renting an apartment in Bloor West Village. After two years of searching for a new house, the couple decided to expand and renovate Dana's existing home.

"To own your own home and land in a desirable community like the South Kingsway is such a luxury," said Dana. "It's a dream for me to be able to stay in a home that I love in a neighbourhood that I adore."

Dana and Kevin were very precise in what they envisioned. They wanted a functional space that suited their lifestyles and interests. They wanted to make this their forever home where they would grow old together.

They wanted their space to be open, beautiful, unique, and inviting which included a large kitchen and dining room to accommodate their extended family. "There will be no kids table at our family Christmas dinner!" Dana exclaimed.

The couple knew that there would be a litany of decisions to make through the project. Understanding that they were too busy to commit the time for all the selections, they required a one-stop-shop design build company to accommodate their needs.

During the summer weekends, they escaped to Kevin's family cottage in Muskoka. During Christmas and March breaks, they flew south to Dana's mother's vacation home in Naples, Florida. Being stuck in appliance and flooring showrooms instead of creating family memories did not appeal to them. My hands-free process did.

Given that the couple knew exactly what they wanted, I asked Kevin how much they planned to invest in the renovation and addition.

"We have a savings of $350,000," he replied. "This should cover everything on our wish list." There was something funny in the way Kevin spoke that made me think he was holding back on his true number. I decided that it was time for an honest conversation with them about costs.

"I hate to break it to you," I said, "but your whole home renovation, along with the expansion, is way more likely to cost in the $700,000 to $800,000 range."

They didn't say anything. They were obviously flabbergasted, so I continued before they could object. "These are realistic numbers that will get you everything on your wish list using qualified professionals to design and build your project legally, obtaining all required permits and getting all required inspections."

"Wow!" said Kevin. "That's a lot more than I thought it would be. I thought it would be half as much."

"Most of our customers don't have the experience or expertise to determine how much renovations of this scope will actually cost," I told him. "After all, most families will renovate only once or twice in their lifetimes. Reality TV shows in particular really create false expectations. Although very entertaining, it's really just that —entertainment! Consider that the featured trades people and suppliers are providing free labour and materials to be on TV, so the stated project costs are a bit skewed. They also don't take into account all of the ancillary costs of doing a project such as design, project management, demolition, job site cleanup, liability insurance, profit and overhead. This is simply the cost of doing business".

I paused to let that sink in, then finished. "In short, you get what you pay for. Half of that amount means half of your wish list."

Kevin didn't like any of what I'd said and was noticeably angry. "You know, I think both families could make do with the house in its current condition and double up in the bedrooms. Kids are used to sharing bedrooms on vacations, anyway."

At that, Dana turned at him. "I have no intention of putting pressure on the kids by robbing them of their privacy and creating resentment among them. This isn't the way I want to start our blended family."

"This could be a really big, expensive mistake," said Kevin. "This project could turn out to be far more expensive, time consuming, and stressful than we imagined. I am just not comfortable proceeding with the renovation!"

Dana rebutted, "Look, I have lived here for 15 years and suffered with no closet space, totally disorganized kitchen with a small eating area and a hideous powder room. My ex-husband and I constantly argued about whether or not to renovate. His stubbornness contributed to our breakup."

He said nothing, and Dana continued. "Kevin, this is important to me so don't fight me on it. I agree, the cost is much higher than I expected, but I also know that even if we sell the house, we won't have enough equity to buy the kind of house we need. I'm tired of us living apart and I want to start living together as soon as possible. The most important thing to me is our happiness and having the family together. Our family is worth it. I don't plan on moving!"

I chimed in. "There's no reason to wait. In fact, if you did, the costs would escalate by 10% per year."

Kevin didn't budge, though, and I left the home that afternoon wondering whether Dana and Kevin would ever come to an agreement. Imagine my surprise when I received a call by Dana the very next day, informing me that they wanted to move forward on the renovation. I asked her how she convinced Kevin. Dana paused before slowly replying.

"After you left, I went upstairs, slipped into my newest Victoria Secret Lingerie, opened a bottle of Merlot, and had a very open discussion with Kevin. It turned out he is just as excited about the project as I am and wants to proceed."

Reality Check

Most people simply don't realize how much a home renovation should cost. Sometimes it's because they base their expectations on what they see on television (transformations done for a song). But home improvement reality TV shows are notorious for unrealistic budgets and little legitimate merit in their acquisition, negotiation and construction processes.

Clients always need a reality check. The shows are scripted, the costs portrayed are unrealistic, and the timelines appear extremely short. The camera doesn't capture the entire story, with most of the drama just for show.

For instance, a typical program might feature a complete main-floor renovation for $35,000 or a high-end kitchen installed for $20,000. The viewer isn't told how that number came to be. Does it include all of the labour, design fees, and materials? Perhaps they're bringing in tradespeople who are doing the work in exchange for exposure, thus bringing down the actual price.

In the real world, things aren't packaged so neatly. In my humble opinion, the costliest mistake a homeowner can make when setting their budget is to lowball the amount of money they have to spend, and hide the actual amount they are prepared to spend. Sometimes they do it because they don't trust the salesperson giving them the quote. They hold back on the number for fear that if the contractor knew the actual amount then it would be spend without question.

A low budget is a dangerous starting point for a customer. Cheaper is not always better. Half the cost can often mean half the value. Beware the verbal contract and the HST-absent cash agreement. As your mother once told you: If it sounds too good to be true, it probably is.

With a low budget, the contractor has to cut every corner possible and, subsequently, ends up cutting quality. With contracts like these, there usually isn't a detailed scope of what is included so the contractor has carte blanche to make choices that may not necessarily be in the interest of the homeowner. An example may be a decision to not hire professional licensed sub-trades to do the electrical and plumbing work, thereby breaking the law.

More importantly, cost-cutting may mean not constructing to code which leads to eliminating a professional inspection of the work. This could create a serious fire or structural hazard. If no permits are obtained, the work is considered illegal. If a Workers Compensation Certificate isn't supplied, a homeowner can be open to a claim by an injured worker. Cutting corners might also include not getting an HVAC engineer to provide a design for ventilation. That could lead to the furnace experiencing backdraft which, in turn, could cause faulty combustion and create invisible but deadly CO_2 gas leaking into the home.

Furthermore, unscrupulous contractors may attempt to extort extra money in the middle of a renovation by refusing to proceed unless another cash payment is made. At this point, the homeowner is helpless and held hostage by the contractor's demands. They either give in or finish the project themselves. This scenario happens too often and, ultimately, turns an exciting project from dream to disaster.

There are numerous unseen costs that make up a good renovation beyond the materials, supplies and labour, such as costs for design, insurance, licenses and proper supervision. Furthermore, it's important for homeowners to expect a swing in their renovation budget and allow for an overrun.

During our meeting, I asked Kevin the source of their savings. He explained that he and Dana had arranged for automatic deductions from their salaries to be put into a savings account.

"Are these tax paid dollars in your savings accounts?" I asked. He said yes.

Do you realize then that you had to earn roughly $700,000 to accumulate $350,000 in net of tax savings? He agreed that yes, of the $700,000 he earned, $350,00 was paid to the government.

This meant his buying power for the savings was actually 50%. To save the required $700,000 for the renovation, he and Dana would have to earn $1.4 million. I suggested they look at the financing through a different lens.

"You borrow on your equity to make more equity," I explained. "Let's compare interest rates. If the interest rate on your loan is between 3 and 4%, and the value of your house is increasing at 10%, that means your home appreciates more than the interest you're paying."

He'd never thought about it that way. I then explained that that if he borrowed the money, they would get 100% buying power for those funds. He nodded.

"Who's going to loan us that kind of money?" he asked.

They had a lot of equity in their existing home and no mortgage. The appraised value of the home, pre-renovation, was $1.5 million. Obtaining a mortgage that carried roughly $3000 per month would be a snap. This way, they use the power of their equity to finance a renovation.

Furthermore, by using their equity, they could create more equity through appreciation. I emphasized the trends in Toronto's housing market. Prices of homes in the last 20 years in Toronto have appreciated by an average of 6.2 to 10% per year according to the Toronto real estate board.

I turned to mortgage broker, Gary Fooks who specializes in funding renovations, to offer some clarity to homeowners who are facing a home renovation and determining how to finance it.

Financing a Renovation 101

Q. Why would I choose a mortgage broker over my neighbourhood banker?

A. Financing a renovation project doesn't have to be a crapshoot. There's a game plan for choosing the best deal. Until recently, borrowing money for a renovation, addition or other home improvement project meant going to the bank and hoping for the best. Today you have many more options. A mortgage broker can offer many more loan options from lenders who are eager to put a loan together to fit your situation and your credit history.

Q. How much can I borrow?

A. To determine your loan amount, lenders use the loan to value ratio which is a percentage of the appraisal value of your home. The usual limit is 80%. Lenders subtract any existing mortgage balance from the amount to arrive at the maximum you can borrow. If you have a good credit rating, the lender might go as high as 85% loan to value.

Q. Where do I get a mortgage?

A. Mortgage shopping starts with mainstream mortgages from banks, credit union, and brokers. Like all mortgages, they use your home as collateral. If you already have a mortgage on your home, you can place a second mortgage behind it. That might sound ominous, but a second mortgage saves you from refinancing your first if you have a very attractive rate.

Q. Can I refinance my existing mortgage

A. One way to take advantage of the appreciation of your home and your increased equity is to refinance your existing mortgage with a new one. There may be penalties and fees. The best option will be to choose a 25-year amortization and spread the cost of the renovation over 25 years.

Q. What is a Home Equity Line of Credit (HELOC)

A. A home equity line of credit is another way to borrow against the value of your home, but unlike a refinance, it doesn't pay off the original mortgage. Instead you get a line of credit usually up to 80% of your home's value, minus the value of any existing home loan. You can add a line of credit to your existing mortgage in order to finance your project without penalties on the existing mortgage. You can draw money down as required and pay interest only on the debt. At the end of the project your bank will be able to route the line of credit into the existing mortgage.

Q. What is a second mortgage?

A. The second mortgage is another way to tap into your equity without refinancing. It is usually provided by private investors who will loan you up to 80% of your construction project. These are short term loans that have to be repaid at the completion of the project. It's more expensive than the first mortgage financing that offers flexibility to complete the project and then obtain a post renovation appraisal. You can use that increased value to refinance your first and pay off your second.

Q. What is construction financing?

A. Construction financing is a loan taken out to pay for the construction cost of a renovation during the construction period. Once the construction is over, the loan amount is repaid through restructuring of the mortgage and refinancing of the mortgage.

Q. What's the best advice you can offer?

A. It is a good idea to set aside 10 to 20% of your project funds to cover items not included in your budget. This includes those options you want to add once construction has begun, such as upgrades, furniture, appliances, window coverings or contingencies. A separate pool of funds lets you make decisions easily without having to renegotiate your financial arrangements.

Q. What's the number one tip for homeowners considering a renovation?

A. Prior to starting to plan a renovation, homeowners should get pre-approved on maximum amount they can borrow on a renovation.

Lastly, don't forget to check out HST rebates, up to $16,000 for renovations.

Don't let the fear of financing prevent you from obtaining the home of your dreams. There are financial options available that make it more possible than most homeowners recognize.

Questions to consider:

- Are you planning to use your savings for your renovation project?

- Did you know you can borrow against your home equity to fund your renovation project?

- Do you understand that if you stay in your renovated home for 10 years you will not only get your money back, but earn a profit?

Conclusion

The Power of Love

"The power of love is a curious thing. Make one man weep, make another man sing. Change a heart to a little white dove. More than a feeling, that's the power of love"

– Huey Lewis, The Power of Love

I hope you enjoyed reading the stories about ordinary families dealing with the stress, frustration, and rewards that come with home improvement projects. As more families decide to make their existing home their forever home, you may also find yourself in a similar predicament. Hopefully, the process to discover your needs and limiting beliefs as they relate to your home may have clarified how you wish to proceed.

You now have the skills to navigate a renovation without suffering some of the setbacks that can accompany such an experience. You are now less likely to experience marital strife or the consequences of choosing the wrong contractor or the wrong time to work with an architect.

Here are my Top 10 Tips on how to become the ideal renovation customer.

1. Maintain a positive attitude and find the humour in each setback.

2. Be open and honest about your project scope and budget.

3. Understand that you get what you pay for when it comes to quality and value.

4. Respect your contractor's advice and rely on his professionalism and experience.

5. Be open-minded regarding new concept designs and materials.

6. Make a commitment to a successful outcome by keeping your eye on the prize.

7. Be decisive when approving designs and selecting materials.

8. Be flexible with your attitude toward delays and rescheduling.

9. Plan a vacation from the renovation to refresh your outlook.

10. Stock up the wine refrigerator.

Renovation is the True Test of Love

Laura and Carl exemplified the most ideal couple to work with through a home renovation. They represented the perfect client in every way.

This couple was fun to be around and were living proof that the honeymoon phase didn't ever have to end. As I got to know them, I found their relationship inspirational. I'd caught Carl, on many occasions, grabbing his wife to give her a big bear hug and kiss. She was always more than happy to receive them. Their relationship was perfect for weathering the storms that can come with a renovation. The plan to move forward with a remodeling was instigated when Laura moved her aging parents into the home. The renovation became a necessity at this point.

We quickly developed a great working relationship. They trusted me and respected my expertise and experience. It was clear from the start that they would rely on my advice and that of my reliable friends and vendors in the business.

When I had the pleasure of first meeting them, they had just celebrated their 25th wedding anniversary and Laura was still showing off the Rolex watch that her husband had given her as she served me a glass of water and lemon. She was clearly enamored with both the watch and her husband.

"I still love him as much today as I did the day we made our vows," Laura said, looking at Carl and smiling.

"That's so nice to hear," I said, somewhat surprised. It wasn't every day that I met couples still devoted to one another after even 10 years, much less 25. She shrugged.

"I guess we got lucky," she said, walking to Carl and giving him a gentle rub on the shoulder. "I know how challenging marriage can be. And, of course, we've had our struggles! Raising three boys isn't easy.

But I could never imagine not having him by my side through all of it."

"Yep," Carl agreed, clearly the less talkative one. "Do you think we've got another 25 years in us?"

"I hope so!" Laura said, laughing. "Though gosh, I don't want to think about how old we'll be then!" She glanced around the kitchen. "And, if we plan to stay put, we'd better fix this house up."

I smiled and nodded my head. The place was dated, for sure. The home was located in an upscale neighbourhood in Oakville. Laura and Carl were the original buyers of the house from the builder 25 years ago. The 5000 square-foot home backed onto a ravine with a walkout basement that opened out to a pool surrounded by mature trees (I'd quickly peeked into the yard before ringing the doorbell). While here, they'd raised three sons, all of whom had attended a nearby private school.

Their home was the backbone of their family's identity and the source of treasured memories. Over the years, the home hosted 25 hockey and soccer banquets, three graduation parties, 175 birthdays, 25 anniversary parties, 25 Christmas celebrations, one engagement party, many heartbreaks, and too many hangovers to mention. This house was the base of the family tree. Of course, over the years it had grown dated in both design and function. The couple recently considered moving but after serious thought and discussions with their grown sons, decided to stay.

Carl was a successful entrepreneur who owned 10 independent pharmacies throughout the GTA. He had a firm grasp of financial issues, having done well with his businesses over the years. The mortgage was paid off and a large retirement fund was in the bank. When we discussed financing the home renovation, he readily agreed that borrowing the equity in his home in order to create more equity made more sense than paying with his own cash.

Once this was established, I arranged a meeting with mortgage broker, Gary Fooks who had years of experience in obtaining renovation funding. Gary provided the couple with pre-approval funding for over $1.5 million and an additional 20% contingency for surprises.

The next step was a meeting with the designers to review the layout. We created concepts that would improve the functionality of the home while updating it to reflect their modern lifestyle.

We started by removing the walls between the kitchen, the dining room and the family room. The new open concept allowed the natural light to shine throughout and enabled family and friends more opportunities to gather for TV, socializing, cooking or working at a laptop.

They needed a little convincing to retire the classic Canadian living room concept. As I'd explained, it had gone the way of the plastic slipcover. The dining room relocated to the living room and the old dining room was transformed into a walk-in pantry and a butler pantry. The modern pantry provided plenty of storage, as well as space for food preparation which kept messes hidden from guests. The pantry was also outfitted with a cooktop and second dishwasher.

The dated stippled ceiling had to go, too. It was replaced with decorative moldings.

The Great Room featured a beautiful fireplace, which we surrounded with custom cabinets that housed the state of art flat screen and sound system by Turtone Electronics .

I thought the picture and sound experience in the Great Room designed by Turtone was as a good as a movie .

The tired old oak staircase was replaced by a beautiful new contemporary set of stairs, and the wood railing was updated with new iron pickets.

To enhance the décor I introduced them to Michael Smith of Royal Lighting who guided them in the selection of beautiful lighting fixtures for the newly renovated rooms.

Engineered wide plank hardwood floors from Aspen Wood Flooring created a contemporary but cozy interior that fit perfectly with the style of the family-oriented home. The front entrance was upgraded with imported porcelain tile from Italy and a new custom door.

With Laura's parents moving in, accommodating their mobility needs was essential. We decided to install a four-stop quiet operating hydraulic elevator with automatic sliding doors.

To help mitigate the clutter that collected over the years, we added storage lockers to the mud room, laundry room, and pantry, and converted one of the five bedrooms into a larger closet for Laura with custom millwork by Komandor Custom Closets. The ensuite bathroom was transformed into a luxury spa by adding a free-standing vessel tub from Cana Roma and a glass shower enclosure.

For the kitchen, I solicited the expertise of my good friend, Horia of Scavolini Kitchens, to create the most ideal design. Their attention to detail is second to none, and given that today's kitchens carry a higher technology price per foot than another other room of the house, I wanted to ensure the best advice in design and appliances. I visited Tasso Appliances to select a Wolf gas burner oven and Sub-zero appliances for the newly designed kitchen.

For beautiful finishing touches, we visited the showroom of Select Marble and Granite. The owner Rento personally helped us choose an outstanding piece of stone for the island top of the backsplash. While plumbing may not sound like the most exciting aspect of a renovation, the showroom at Cana Roma would convince anyone otherwise. We ended up selecting a number of beautiful imported fixtures for the kitchen and bathrooms to add a wow factor.

It was decided to replace all of the windows of the home with new triple glazed, state-of-the-art energy efficient windows from Château windows.

As a special treat to Laura and Carl I introduced them to my good friend Elizabeth, who is the owner of the iconic furniture store Elizabeth Interiors. She completed the décor with fabulous furniture and that created an elegant but comfortable home.

As expected, Laura and Carl were easy to get along with the entire process. There were a few delays that would rattle most couples, but they took it all in stride. When the design was complete, they were thrilled with the results.

At the party they'd hosted to celebrate the new home, the couple had sent out invitations that read "Come help us celebrate the next 25 years!" Now that's love.

The True Power of Love

At the beginning of this book, I predicted that fewer than 10% of readers would break through the terror barrier, take action, and proceed with the renovation project. You've already read about the various reasons that motivate a person to renovate. Perhaps you struggled with your own decision on whether or not to go forward with it, unable to reach a clear understanding of why, exactly, you would renovate in the first place.

Completing a home renovation can be one of life's most satisfying events. The day you finally sit down after all the hammering is over and say "it's done and I love it," will be the most memorable moment of your life as a homeowner.

What makes a homeowner embark on the roller coaster renovation journey?

The answer is simple: Love.

The address by US bishop Michael Bruce at Prince Harry and Meghan Markle's's Royal Wedding perfectly sums up the power of love. He quoted Dr. Martin Luther King when he announced that "we must discover the power of love, the redemptive power of love. And when we discover that, we will be able to make of this old world a new one. Love is the only way."

There is power in love!

The story of Meghan Markel is a Cinderella fairytale. A commoner marries the prince. Who would have thought that the power of love could modernize the monarchy by breaking through the exclusive social norms and traditions of the British aristocracy and establishment to enable an American divorced woman of mixed race to marry a prince in line to be king?

Likewise, it is the power of love the drives and motivates homeowners to put up with all the hassles of a renovation project. It takes love to modernize your home!

Why do homeowners renovate?

For the love of themselves

For the love of a husband

For the love of a wife

For the love of one's children, family and friends

For the love of one's home and neighbourhood

For the love of design

For the love of new products and features

For the love of entertaining family and friends

When homeowner discovers that the power of love is why they're renovating, homeowners will do anything to make it happen.

I'll leave you with a poem that sums it all up:

It takes hands to build a house, but only hearts can build a home.

Gene Maida.

OTHER RESOURCES

Book Suggestions

Tony Robbins

What Do You Believe: 16 Limiting Beliefs That Are Preventing You From Thriving

Unleash Your Power

Mel Robbins

The 5 Second Rule

Linda Petrin

Define your Life Design your Home

Paco Underhill

What Women Want

Cloe Mandes

Relationship Breakthrough

Abraham Maslow

A Theory of Human Motivation

Podcast Suggestions

Tony Robbins – *3 Steps to a Breakthrough*

Personality Hacker – *Overcoming Limiting Beliefs*

PREFERRED VENDORS DIRECTORY

Design Builder
Georgian Renovations

Description For decades, Georgian has been custom renovating homes with unparalleled craftsmanship. Specializing in additions, renovations, and complete home transformations, the process is meticulous form start to finish, with their signature, one-of-a-kind flare for design, and the comfort of a five-year warranty and fixed-price guarantee.

p: 905.405.7276 | e: info@georgianreno.com
1175 Meyerside Drive, Suite 2 Mississauga, ON

Stone Tops
Select Granite Tops Inc.

Select Granite Tops Inc. is a fabricator of natural stone (granite, marble, quartzite, onyx, semi-precious and soapstone) and man-made materials (quartz, porcelain, ultra compact, solid surface and micro crystal stone). They offer custom templating, precision manufacturing, professional installation and after service support.

p: 905.879.5000 | e: sales@selectgranitetops.com
5-225 McNaughton Road East Vaughan, ON

Plumbing
Cana Roma

Canaroma's 20,000 square foot designer showroom features an array of bath, lighting and tile products including exclusive designer lines. Canaroma stands as the only authorized dealer in Canada currently carrying the highly-exclusive internationally renown brands which include Artelinea, Aquos, Glass Design, Oasis, Onsen, Macral, NOVA, Armadi Art, Cerasa, Vissoni, Sherle Wagner, Treesse and Windisch. In addition, Canaroma has the largest boutique in Canada for Dornbracht, THG and Porcelanosa oor and wall tiles. Canaroma offers modern vanities, contemporary vanities, traditional vanities, double sink vanities, pedestal basins, glass vanities, luxury vanities, shower columns, shower glass panels, shower bases, round toilets, 1 piece toilets, 2 piece toilets, as well as kitchen/bath faucets and bath accessories.

p: 905.856.7979 | e: info@canaroma.com
7979 Weston Road Vaughan, ON

Mortgage Broker
Gary Fooks, 8TWELVE Mortgage Corporation

Gary believes that every customer deserves the best care and service when purchasing or refinancing the home of their dreams. He can place all types of mortgages including purchases, refinances, equity takeouts, debt consolidations, renewals and mortgages for self-employed.

p: 1 877-812-8128 | e: gary@8Twelve.Mortgage
45 Sheppard Ave. E, Suite 211, Toronto, ON M2N5W9

European Kitchens
Scavolini Toronto Showroom

For fifteen years, Scavolini Toronto has been Greater Toronto's go-to source for the latest trends and the finest quality in custom-designed Italian kitchens. In addition to world-renowned Scavolini kitchens, they offer Scavolini bathrooms, as well as fittings, furniture and accessories for every room in the house, from closets to hallways to offices, for a coherent design and consistent living experience.

p: 416 961-2929
1330 Castlefield Ave, Toronto, ON M6B 4B3

Windows & Doors
Chateau Window and Door Systems

Windows and doors are integral to the overall design and aesthetic of your home. At Chateau Window & Door Systems we aim to converge elegant design with the utmost efficiency and functionality, to achieve a polished look and optimal performance.

p: 417.783.3916 | e: info@chateauwindows.com
90 Tycos Dr., Suite #1, Toronto, ON

Furniture
The Art Shoppe

The Art Shoppe features the finest home furnishing collections from around the world. From living room, dining room and bedroom furniture to accents, including fine art, rugs, throw pillows, and lighting, the Art Shoppe is the best source for luxury furniture.

p: 416.487.3211 | e: info@theartshoppe.com
71 Kincort Street, Toronto, ON

Flooring
Aspen Wood Floors

Aspen Wood Floors is a leading distributor of quality hardwood floors; solid & engineered hardwood, domestic & exotic, as well as cork flooring, bamboo, laminate, vinyl and carpeting to the Greater Toronto Areas.

p: 905.281.2900 | e: sales@aspenwoodfloors.com
505 Queensway East, Mississauga, ON

Furniture
Decorium

Decorium have continued to be the leaders when it comes to value, style, and selection. They constantly change and have new and fresh products in our showroom weekly. Experience a unique way of shopping for home furnishing at Decorium.

p: 416.736.6120 | e: shoponline@decorium.ca
363 Supertest Rd, North York, ON

Elizabeth Interiors

The Elizabeth Interiors brand has several unique, leading retail locations catering to the decor needs of our clientelle. Our furniture and decor showrooms proudly resource over 500 of the most elite furniture companies in the world.

p: 905.333.6670 | w: elizabethinteriors.com
3225 Fairview Street, Burlington, ON

Lighting
Union Lighting

Union Lighting and Furnishings is Canada's largest lighting showroom and offers a comprehensive collection of fine furniture and decorative accessories. Union caters to both homeowners and trade professionals in their 100,000 square foot building located in the heart of the Castlefield Design District in Toronto.

p: 416.652.2200 | e: info@unionlf.com
1491 Castlefield Avenue, Toronto, ON

Appliances
Tasco

With a main focus on appliances, Tasco Appliances quickly became Ontario's appliance retailer of choice, specializing in high-end appliances. We were able to expand upon our largely builder-based clientele evolving into a retail outlet for Toronto's discerning homeowners.

p: 905.421.0367 | e: sales@tasco.net
1095 Kingston Rd, North York, ON

Rugs
Weaver's Art

Serving Interior Designers & Architects with the largest inventory of fine area rugs in Canada. Weaver's Art specialize in hand-knotted silk & wool area rugs.

p: 416.929.7929 | w: weaversart.com
1400 Castlefield Avenue, Toronto, ON

Electronics
Trutone

Trutone ensure that the smart solutions we specify and install perfectly complement your home, office or leisure space. As certified dealers of the best manufacturers, Trutone can specify the system to perfectly fit how you live, work or play.

p: 905.270.3440 | e: sales@trutone.ca
980 Dundas Street East, Mississauga, ON

Closets & Cabinetry
Komandor

Komandor makes Toronto's highest quality closets, sliding doors, and custom cabinetry. Our products set the industry standard for quality, performance, durability and added value because we oversee every aspect of their design, production and installation.

p: 905.766.0880 | e: info@komandor.ca
863 Rangeview Road, Mississauga, ON

Lighting
Royal Lighting

Royal Lighting have the best prices while always adding new products to our selection (average 100 new items per month). Their selection and service make them the ideal showroom in Canada for all of your lighting needs.

p: 416.782.1129 | w: royallighting.com
1549 Avenue Road, Toronto, ON

Landscaping
Cedar Springs

For over 30 years, Cedar Springs has been creating stunning resort-quality landscapes right here in Southern Ontario neighbourhoods. We take great satisfaction in the craftsmanship we deliver, but also in the experiences our spaces provide for homeowners.

Creating five-star, resort–like landscapes is also about the level of service you can expect from our staff. When you use Cedar Springs, you're working with a highly professional, people-oriented company that aims to please. From the initial call with one of our sales/design reps, to the crew member that sweeps up your drive at the end of the day, we know your experience will be first rate.

p: 905.333.6789 | e: info@cedarsprings.net
3242 South service Road West, Oakville, ON

Movers
AMJ Campbell

Moving your home stress-free from start to finish.

At AMJ Campbell, we have been helping Canadians with their home moving needs for over 80 years, dedicated to providing exceptional, personalized service. Together we have figured out how to plan and execute a seamless, stress-free move. Let the experts at AMJ Campbell handle the details, so you can focus on settling into your new home.

A Home Moving Consultant will come to you at your convenience, assess your needs, explain all procedures, identify any concerns, and assist with the smallest detail.

Call us at 1-888 AMJ MOVE (265-6683)

Heating & Cooling
Four Seasons Air Control

Since 1991 Four Seasons Air Control has been providing exceptional service as a licensed full service HVAC company. With over 12,000 customers, we're known for our commitment, passion, technical expertise and our ability to provide our customers with tailored solutions that meet their needs. We listen, and we pay attention to the all-important details. And we always care about what matters to you. Precision, consistency, performance, long-standing relationships... all of this describes who we are.

Kevin Katabchi | p: 416.410.2473 or 905.795.0982 ext 222
e: info@komandor.ca | w: fourseasonsac.ca
1050 Britannia Road E, Unit # 1, Mississauga, ON

Hotel X Toronto

The new Hotel X Toronto by Library Hotel Collection is more than just your ordinary hotel in Toronto. With innovative offerings in entertainment, accommodations, athletics, and dining, our luxury urban oasis featuring resort-style amenities—the only hotel of its kind in Downtown Toronto—is the epitome of inviting hospitality, with a focus on sustainability and the greater Toronto community.

It's about you. It's about the view.

Learn more at **HotelXToronto.com**